# Not Just
# Ordinary
# Young
# Men &
# Young
# Women

## BOOKS AUTHORED OR CO-AUTHORED
## BY ELAINE CANNON

*Adversity*

*As a Woman Thinketh*

*Baptized and Confirmed: Your Lifeline to Heaven*

*Be a Bell Ringer*

*Bedtime Stories for Grownups*

*Boy of the Land, Man of the Lord*

*Corner on Youth*

*Eight is Great*

*The Girl's Book*

*God Bless the Sick and Afflicted*

*Heart to Heart*

*Life—One to a Customer*

*Love You*

*Merry, Merry Christmases*

*The Mighty Change*

*Mothers and "Other Mothers"*

*Putting Life in Your Life Story*

*The Seasoning*

*The Summer of My Content*

*The Time of Your Life*

*Turning Twelve or More: Living by the Articles of Faith*

# Not Just Ordinary Young Men & Young Women

## Elaine Cannon

BOOKCRAFT
Salt Lake City, Utah

Library of Congress Catalog Card Number: 91–73286
ISBN 0–88494–809–9

First Printing, 1991

Printed in the United States of America

*NJO  NJO  NJO  NJO  NJO  NJO  NJO  NJO  NJO  NJO*

How beautiful is youth!
how bright it gleams
With its illusions,
aspirations, dreams!
Book of Beginnings,
Story without End,
Each maid a heroine,
and each man a friend!

. . . . . . . . . . . . . . . . .

All possibilities
are in its hands,
No danger daunts it,
and no foe withstands.

—Longfellow

# Contents

NJO NJO NJO NJO NJO NJO NJO NJO NJO NJO

# *Inside Info*

This book is to help you grow up wonderful.

This book will share secrets reserved for you, such as how to make the most out of what you have to work with; the pluses, the strengths, and the miseries of your time of life; and your place in the history of mankind.

These are tough times—the most stressful ever— the most demanding of your inner strength and mind-set.

Your life is cloaked in the wonders of technology; of color and environment; of variety in style, entertainment, food, media; of shrinking boundaries between countries, age-groups, cultures, religious beliefs.

Reach back through this incredible unfolding to find your orientation to Christ. He is your Savior, and few but you are positive of this. The impact of such knowledge is one part of what makes you "not just ordinary young men and women."[1] It sets the tone for the purpose of your life.

*NJO   NJO   NJO   NJO   NJO   NJO   NJO   NJO   NJO   NJO*

This book is designed to help you be what you want and need to be.

## How to Use This Book

Well, you could settle for using it to press flowers from your sister's wedding, your first date, your youth trip to Nauvoo.

You could flip through the book. Skim through to the ending. Settle for that.

Spot read. Make an abridgment, so you can say you are familiar with the highlights. Highlight the highlights.

Read the beginning and ending of each chapter.

Browse for stories, saving your reading of the solid counsel until you have to give a talk or teach a lesson.

But for best results:

Start at the first and read your way through to the last line. Find out what is in the book, why it is especially for **not just ordinary** Young Men and Young Women.

Study the contents page. You'll get more out of any book if you follow the format or the map or the user's guide.

Mark the parts that work for you. Underline, outline, highlight, circle those sections that leap from the page into your thinking. Color the gospel truths, principles, scripture quotations that bolster your own beliefs. Checkmark the new-to-you ideas.

Look up in a good dictionary the words you don't know. Go back and read again those lines that offer very clear direction for your particular life.

Pray for guidance to understand those things that will benefit you spiritually and mentally, socially as well.

*NJO  NJO  NJO  NJO  NJO  NJO  NJO  NJO  NJO  NJO*

Look for answers to your particular problems. When you see your challenges as growing experiences, as part of a developmental journey, there won't be so much pain connected with learning.

Concentrate as you read, trying to focus on ways to apply truth to your life and times. This book can help you keep your mind on your own business, your goal, your immediate calling, your ultimate mission.

## Your Ultimate Mission

You can get a transplant today for almost any body part—cornea, liver, kidney, heart, bald head! I know a doctor who performed a miracle measure to provide a teenage girl with tear ducts—not just so she could cry during the mushy movies, but so she could see. No tear ducts means no moisture, which means no vision. As her eyelids blinked (as our eyelids do countless times during a day), it was dry surface rubbing against dry surface, and scar tissue formed, blocking her vision. Like your soft winter hand getting calloused on a summer rake or hoe.

The answer? A saliva duct. Now, keep in mind that a saliva duct can only be seen with a powerful magnifying lens. The girl's doctor managed the operation by working inside her mouth as far as possible—getting the lens in place, finding a proper duct, and then running it up inside her cheek and alongside her nose under the skin. The all-important hole in the corner of each eye was created, the saliva duct attached, and—presto chango! voila!—a tear duct! The only problem was that every time she saw a pickle she cried!

There are transplants that work in the place of originals—artificial or man-made pieces of the body

*NJO NJO NJO NJO NJO NJO NJO NJO NJO NJO*

that work like the real thing or just look something like the real thing.

Tinted contact lenses change eye color. Wigs enhance natural hair. A prosthesis replaces a limb. A multi-pronged hook serves as a hand. Incredible.

But for life—your life—it is one chance to live. Nothing to look like it or perform like it. This is it—your turn on Earth's turf.

Your ultimate mission—regardless of details in filling such a mission—is to help Jesus Christ in his mission. His mission, you recall, is to bring to pass the immortality and eternal life of man, woman, and child.

When Jesus was not far from your age—twelve years old, according to the Bible—he was found at last by his worried parents, who had become separated from him on a journey. Jesus was teaching wise men at the temple. "Wist ye not that I must be about my Father's business?" he asked his father and mother. (See JST, Luke 2:42–49.)

You can be sure your parents want you to be about your ultimate mission, too. So do your leaders, teachers, and caring friends and family. So do I. This book will help you prepare to help others.

Life on earth, as you well know, is about that preparation for all the rest of forever. If you want to go where God is, you have to make it through this life in proper spiritual condition. It's a fact that on that last walk through the veil all you can take with you from earth is your *as is* spirit.

This book will help you polish up yours!

## Why Talk of Death When You Are So Alive?

Imagine checking in with God when you haven't even made it all the way through the Book of Mormon,

NJO NJO NJO NJO NJO NJO NJO NJO NJO NJO

and you still poke, jab, tease, and taunt your little brother and/or sister.

Why talk about death when you are just beginning to live? You'll quickly see why if you read the obits, check the stats in the daily news. People may die when they are babies, kids, teenagers, young parents. In some cases they die when they least expect it. The only ones who seem ready to die are old people who are stricken in body and mind, lonely for long-gone loved ones; and they wait and wait and wait.

Sometimes young people assume they are not mortal—that they are forever alive no matter how fast they drive or how crazy they act, experimenting with this and that forbidden fruit.

Actually everyone should genuinely live until they die, and they should live as if they might die right away. Repentance is a great principle; but you can waste a lot of time, take a dangerous chance with forever, if you live and sin on the basis that you can repent *someday*.

My files are full of stories about people who had nurtured that mistaken idea. And guess what? That *someday* didn't come in time before the funeral. This book can give you powerful reasons and helpful guidance for living so that death, one day, will be welcome.

## Inside This Book

Inside this book you will find:

- what makes you **not just ordinary** Young Men and Young Women
- some gripping details of the no-nonsense lifestyle
- who your Best Friend is on earth and in heaven

*NJO NJO NJO NJO NJO NJO NJO NJO NJO NJO*

- the truth about today's trends—from sass to sex
- a look at the hokum about hormones, and the dignity in doing the right thing
- that chastity is its own reward—like honesty
- that lying makes you a liar and a loser; that lying is a needless net around your freedom
- the secret behind meaningful relationships
- that self-esteem comes from knowing who you really are
- how to be a survivor through disappointment, dumb mistakes, dreamy success
- the importance of knowing the way to talk with God
- info about when to hold your tongue, control your temper, stand firm
- what to do instead of "getting even" or "giving in"
- where comfort comes from
- what you can believe and whom you can believe
- what to do about family problems, sibling rivalry, and cramped quarters
- a list of absolutes and the truth about "laws irrevocably decreed in heaven"

## For the Strength of You Not Just Ordinary Young Men and Young Women

Here and now, inside these covers, right on these pages you will find all this information and inspiration and more for strength in your youth. And you need spiritual strength, because you **not just ordinary** Young Men and Young Women are targets of Satan. Satan does operate in this world and is as real as

*NJO NJO NJO NJO NJO NJO NJO NJO NJO NJO*

Jesus. Satan desires to sift you as wheat chaff in the wind. He wants to curl your sail, strip your saplings, block your moves, trip up your brisk walk, puncture your personal progress, and thwart your best efforts.

Satan wants to turn you from **not just ordinary** Young Men and Young Women to pitiful peers in a lost cause. He wants to render you ineffective. He wants you to be miserable sinners.

This must not happen to you. Read this book, for inside it is information to help you grow up wonderful!

*NJO  NJO  NJO  NJO  NJO  NJO  NJO  NJO  NJO  NJO*

*Youth is particularly designed for . . .*

earning, eating,

laughing, loving,

helping,

playing,

praying, shoveling,

learning, testing,

teasing, tending,

serving, sliding,

dancing, mending,

hiking, racing,

reading, repenting,

creating, clowning,

snacking, shouting,

cycling, coaxing, sleeping,

doubting,

getting,

giving,

gathering, surprising and

growing up wonderful!

# CHAPTER
## 1

# *Not Just Ordinary*

## *Not Just Ordinary*

T-shirts today are a favorite art form and occasionally a quaint source for truth. There is one that shows an addicted grizzly bear gnashing his teeth and growling, "Bring me some chocolate and nobody gets hurt."

Well, nobody gets hurt much, either, when *you* spread your own kind of sweetness. I know because I have watched you in action for a lot of years. Oh, how you have sweetened my life, too!

Across the earth and back again, God has permitted me to rub shoulders and cross hearts with you and others like you, with your parents and leaders. What a time I have had watching you, marveling over you, learning from you! You have learned while young to have high hope, to put your trust in God, and to stir up shining moments for those around you. What a difference you've made in your particular world and beyond! What help you have been saving lives—physically and spiritually!

Soft soap?

Yes, soft soap. But you deserve it!

From the Philippines to Cartagena, from Sydney to Stuttgart, from Taiwan to Tennessee, from Nova Scotia to Seoul, there are stories to be told about teenagers connected with the "Boost and Beacon Platoon." I traveled and taught and talked and made notes.

Here are some examples I noted of **not just ordinary** Young Men and Young Women.

## Montana

In Great Falls, Montana, a youth conference was concluding with testimony time. The young people moved forward to the front row of the chapel to wait for their turn. Things went along well for a time, and then all of a sudden a good-looking guy in spiffy garb surprised us by standing up back in the center section of the congregation. As an editor for the Church youth magazine I knew a good story was happening. I grabbed my pencil and notebook:

"I'm sorry for speaking out of turn. I hadn't intended to say anything, but. . . ."

It was a surprise he was speaking at all!

For the long weekend he had done little else but stand around and look at everyone. All the girls yearned to dance with him, but he hugged a post, watching. The boys needed him for team play, but he only leaned against the bleachers and checked it all out. During the workshops he sat in a corner alone, though listening. He played it cool. The problem was he had his act together, a leader type with a store-window-put-together appearance. He stood out from the crowd, all right, and he wouldn't mix. Now he was talking.

*NJO   NJO   NJO   NJO   NJO   NJO   NJO   NJO   NJO   NJO*

"I live in a branch where there aren't many girls. Oh, there are little Primary girls and big, comfortable Relief Society ladies, but there aren't any Mormon [pause] girls." He moved his hands in the shape of a girl's figure. Everyone laughed and listened. A mystery was about to unfold.

The boy continued: "I came to this conference so that I could see what a real Mormon girl looks like. And I've been looking [Oh, they knew he had been looking, just looking!], and I've seen Mormon girls who are wholesome and Mormon girls who are a little far-out and into trends. I've seen girls who cling to guys and other girls who cluster together like bees on a sweet orange blossom. Well, I've decided that a Mormon girl is a many-splendored thing. You see, a Mormon girl has . . . well, uh, a Mormon girl is . . . I mean, a Mormon girl looks . . ." He stuttered a bit. Here was this boy who had only looked and now was overcome with emotion at what he'd seen. Of course he had everyone's attention. He was fascinating, the cutest boy there, and he surely was going to say something wonderful.

"A Mormon girl is the most . . . Hey! [clapping his hands together and smiling brightly at his good idea] I'll tell you what. Let's all go get married in the temple."

It was startling. Caught off guard, there was hardly a girl in the place who didn't want to "pied piper" behind him to the nearest temple. Polygamy never looked so good.

What was his magic?

Looking the part. Being interested in everything and everyone. Setting himself apart from the thundering herds. Watching, learning. Putting a value on quality in God's terms. Now he summed up the secret of

NJO NJO NJO NJO NJO NJO NJO NJO NJO NJO

living. This boy with high standards came right to the point: Find the right girl (or boy) and get on with the good life.

## Taiwan

While I was the Church's general president of the Young Women I visited Taiwan. In Taipei the youth chorus behind the podium provided inspiring music for the visit of general Church officers from Salt Lake City, Utah. I was overcome with joy as I studied row after row of attractive, fresh-looking, black-haired Young Men and Young Women. They were the chosen generation of Taiwan. They listened intently to every speaker and sang their hearts out on cue.

When it was time for us to leave, the President of The Church of Jesus Christ of Latter-day Saints turned toward this practiced chorus and waved his white handkerchief so they could pick him out of the pressing crowd. It was stunning to see an all-inclusive change come over that group. It was as if a signal had been given, as if a water tap had been turned on. Tears streamed down the cheeks of every boy and girl as they waved back. What joy! They knew they were in the presence of a prophet of God. They *knew* that this man was the mouthpiece of God on earth at this time. All of us knew that they knew, and we began weeping as well.

## University City, USA

When I was the youth editor for the *Deseret News* I spent a lot of time listening to troubled teenagers. Marissa was one of them. She had lived for a time in a big city with a large university at its hub. She had dropped out of school after the first quarter and worked in the food services to earn money for the next round. She was the salad-and-steak-bar girl who catered to athletes. She was pretty and feminine, with a personality to match. Naturally the school's athletic heroes were attracted to her. They dished up their male charm while she dished up mixed greens. It was a losing game for Marissa, because the flirting that started out in fun ultimately ended up in childbirth.

Marriage was not an option so the first major decision was whether to allow the pregnancy to go forward. Marissa opted to reject abortion. When she came back home to have the baby, we spent a lot of time counseling together.

The second, and maybe the toughest, decision was made after hours of talking matters over, together with her parents. Should she keep the baby or give it up? She decided to give up the baby for adoption.

The final decision was choosing the adoptive parents. Marissa wanted to have some say in this, even though she wouldn't actually know the names of the adoptive families being considered.

We agreed about the likelihood that Heavenly Father would be interested in where that spirit child of his would be placed. This has been my experience with countless cases of unwed mothers and illegitimate babies.

(Time out for an opinion: I use the term *illegitimate* even though the world has largely abandoned it. I believe we should tell it like it is. We should remind young people who offend-in-love that fooling around out of wedlock can bring into the world babies that are outside legal family status. Illegitimate. This is too high a price to pay—for the child, the unwed mother, responsible grandparents, and for other youth who see the poor example. One day more of the culpable boys may start suffering, too when they understand more clearly their own part in such a situation.)

Marissa did a lot of praying during that period of time. A month or so later she came back to see me. She brought with her pictures of her baby taken at birth and a copy of the letter she had written to leave with the adoptive mother until the appropriate day for the child to receive it in later years.

Then she shared special feelings with me about the whole heartbreaking experience. She was glad she had prayed a lot about where that baby was placed. It kept her close to Heavenly Father. It led her to true repentance and an unselfish desire to do what was right for this newborn. She was thankful that she had asked for a bishop's blessing as she went into labor. Her mother had asked for one, too, that she might support her daughter in the decision to give the child for adoption.

"I gave up my life, for her," explained Marissa. "At least I gave her up so that she could have the best possible chance. Some people feel as if they own their offspring. But after talking with you I came to really understand that she wasn't my baby at all, ever. I made a mistake and I paid a price for it. But that's no reason for the baby to suffer.

"You know, I finally felt forgiven. The Spirit flooded over me when I made a firm decision about the adoptive family and I carefully signed the papers. I felt akin to the Savior, who gave up his life for us. I sacrificed for the baby that she might have a good life. I have no regrets or adjustments now, you see. I didn't 'give up' my baby. I took every prayerful precaution I could to make a blessing out of a mess. I wasn't a bad girl, you see," she explained. "I was a good girl gone wrong, and I had to make up for it."

*NJO  NJO  NJO  NJO  NJO  NJO  NJO  NJO  NJO  NJO*

Actually, when questioned later, Marissa admitted it would have been a good idea for her to have prayed as hard for her own life as she did for her baby's—and to have done so earlier. Maybe then she wouldn't have suffered this heartache at all.

## The Philippine Islands

On the outskirts of Manila I arrived at a little chapel just in time to see a line of deacons quietly waiting in front of the door to the bishop's office. There was no pushing, shoving, poking, pulling, nudging, knocking, jostling, or giggling. The boys didn't talk. They stood there reverently waiting as the bishop handed out clean white shirts for each boy to wear while passing the sacrament. When the meeting was over the boys stood in line again before the bishop and removed the shirts, carefully handing them back.

You see, the families are so poor in that sector that they didn't have suitable clothing for church, let alone white shirts for passing the sacrament. Those boys were thrilled with the privilege of looking the proper part to serve the Lord in reverence.

Of course most of you are very reverent in church, too. We just can't tell because of all the lack of reverence around you!

## Utah

Our family-owned shop The Dressmaker, in Foothill Village, was a hub for girls and their mothers to come to for fabric and design ideas for proms, weddings, Sunday-best dresses. One day I was measuring yardage for two girls who attended a private Catholic

NJO NJO NJO NJO NJO NJO NJO NJO NJO NJO

school nearby. Over at the pattern corner a mother and her daughter, Stacey, sat arguing over formal patterns. Stacey was nearly out of control. Her mother wouldn't agree to a strapless formal design. The young woman raised her voice, using words like *stupid, archaic, kindergarten frocks.* The mother held her ground, talking about Church standards, and the teenage girl groaned loudly, "Oh, Mother!" It was clear that the young woman was not only living in the world but partaking of it heavily.

The two other customers and I couldn't help but hear the argument and witness the tantrum. The shop was not large. But when Stacey came crying over to the counter, the two girls from the Catholic boarding school took things out of my hand. "I couldn't help overhearing your fight with your mom," one of them said to Stacey. "Come on. What difference does the style make? Get a new dress, go to your dance, and smile a lot." She was practical.

Then the other one spoke. "Look. You are a Mormon girl. I am a Catholic one. You think you have the only restrictions? Forget it. It's called growing up safe. At our school we can't even wear anything sleeveless, let alone strapless. Even if we defy the rules, it doesn't get us anywhere; the sisters have a box by the door at the dance—a box full of jackets and scarves to shroud us with if our formals aren't modest enough. Hey, we've survived. We're seniors. We're happy. Come on, kid, don't hassle your mom. I just wish I could be home with mine to hear her approval when I leave for the dance."

Stacey didn't say thanks to the girls, but she did quit crying and bought the pattern her mother had approved.

I've thought a lot about that incident. Sometimes

*NJO   NJO   NJO   NJO   NJO   NJO   NJO   NJO   NJO   NJO*

the **not just ordinary** youth haven't been baptized—
yet. Sometimes Church membership doesn't insure
stalwart youth; it should, but there is that matter of
agency—one must *choose* to listen, to learn, to obey.

## Toronto

In Toronto we stood in a reception line to greet
youth who had come from all over the province for a
series of events geared particularly to strengthen
them. These **not just ordinary** Young Men and Young
Women were breathless with excitement and bur-
dened with personal belongings stuffed in everything
from pillowcases to cardboard boxes. Watching them
was like seeing the tide come in. The sacrifice to get
there had bolstered their anticipation and brought
forth the Holy Spirit in rich measure. Love and laugh-
ter, memories and future plans marked their greetings.

It was time for the weekend's opening exercises to
begin when suddenly four boys came bursting into the
church. They were hard to recognize under the soil of
long travel. They were weak and weary of body because they had had little food during two days on the
road. But smiles on their radiant faces reassured me
there was a light from within. What was their story?
What made them **not just ordinary** youth?

They had ached to be part of that youth conference.

They had no money.

No one else from their area was going to the conference.

They were determined not to give up.

These boys were resourceful and prayerful. They
would "pioneer" their way to Toronto, a long haul but

worth it. They found some discarded car wheels. They scrounged reject lumber. And they built a rugged handcart to hold their few belongings and to take turns resting in.

It worked! They pulled and shoved that handcart the four hundred miles to the meeting place! Just to hear the word of the Lord and mingle with people who were trying to be true disciples.

As speakers we rose to the occasion in order to reward these exemplary and resourceful boys. As listeners the conference participants drank spiritual refreshment and bolstered their own commitment after the example of these four special peers.

## Temple Square

5:30 A.M. October general conference time. Bitter cold with gathering clouds. Crowds already filled the alcove doors around the outside of the fat, squat, oval, historic Tabernacle, built by pioneers and now welcoming a new vanguard.

I had convinced our Church magazine photographer that he would be able to take some wonderful pictures of devoted Saints from New Zealand, Fiji, England, South America, and "All Points to Wherever" while they waited to get seats inside the building. What a story we'd have for the Church magazines! I was right.

We introduced ourselves and interviewed various interesting-looking people, and responded to the promptings of the Spirit to select others. Suddenly I was drawn to a young woman who was heavily braced on her legs and back. Her arms were supported by special grips on her crutches. She was pretty, and cold!

*NJO   NJO   NJO   NJO   NJO   NJO   NJO   NJO   NJO   NJO*

But there she stood, shivering in line. My heart turned over.

We made arrangements to get her a seat inside at once. As we talked I asked where her coat was—did I need to find one for her before the conference was over? I thought she might have traveled from some warm clime and neglected to pack a coat.

"No," she laughed, "I have a coat in the parked car. It's just that I can't handle crowds, crutches, and a coat. So I had to make a value judgment."

When I found out that she was only from Provo, Utah, forty-five miles or so south of Salt Lake City, I asked her why she didn't stay home, where she could watch conference in warmth and comfort.

"Oh, Sister Cannon, I wouldn't miss being here for all the comfort in the world. It's different being *here.* You see, I just love to be in the company of people who are willing to make a sacrifice to hear the word of the Lord."

## Office of the Prophet, Church Headquarters

It was a high point in Church service for me to sit on a small sofa with President Spencer W. Kimball and a beautiful, caring young woman who had completed a great service for others like her.

She was young and she was blind. She was so hungry to participate in the full Church program for young women that she set about the task of translating into braille the official materials. The two-year task of translation had been accomplished with the help of her peers and a devoted Young Women leader, who read to her as she entered the information in braille.

NJO NJO NJO NJO NJO NJO NJO NJO NJO NJO

When the project was completed, we arranged for her to meet the prophet and make an official presentation of the first volume to him.

"Look, President Kimball," she said. "Here is your name in Braille." She took his hand and fingered the raised symbols of the special alphabet for the blind that spelled his name. "Can you feel that?"

"So you have put my name in braille, have you?" he said. "Well, just so you don't take my name in vain!" How we laughed together over that! It was reward enough for this lovely, diligent girl.

## Halifax, Nova Scotia

On one occasion I was touring a mission during February when ice and snow storms had bombarded the New England area near the Canadian border. On the day we were to fly to Nova Scotia, the sun came out and began melting the snow from the deep piles on each side of the shoveled walk from the runway to the terminal. When our chartered plane landed, the sun was setting, and the dropping temperatures of that north country had already turned wet walks into sheets of ice. Airport personnel hadn't kept up with nature by salting the area. It was treacherous.

I was first off the plane and unaware of the problem. I had taken just a few steps before I slipped, fell backwards, and banged my head, suffering a concussion as well as cracking three vertebrae in my neck.

There were many marvelous things about that experience, but what truly touched me was the faith and practical help of those youth involved in the area. When they learned of my plight they moved into action. Over three hundred of them canvassed the homes and businesses in the New England mission, selling

*NJO   NJO   NJO   NJO   NJO   NJO   NJO   NJO   NJO   NJ*

chocolate bars at a profit. They raised an incredible amount of money to help with medical expenses occasioned by the accident and with a subsequent necessary lawsuit.

There was a swell of excitement when they made the presentation to me weeks later. They had jokes to tell and posters of presentation, tributes and skits. A fervent prayer . . . and the big check!

We all laughed and cried together at this culmination of incredible personal sacrifice and caring by these **not just ordinary** Young Men and Young Women. I was touched by their quality and unselfishness, their hard work and their good humor, as well as their generosity. And I don't know what I would have done without help from these **not just ordinary** Young Men and Young Women.

## Rose Bowl, Southern California

Thousands of people jammed the Rose Bowl to witness and participate in an ambitious undertaking of a dance spectacular. I was one of the special guests from Salt Lake City and serving as general president of the Young Women of the Church.

In my best white dress I marched to the beat of the band across the playing field in the stadium where the famous Rose Bowl games take place. Behind me marched one thousand twelve- and thirteen-year-old girls, also dressed in their best white outfits. Each carried her "Banner before the Lord" on tall poles. Each girl had made a banner as part of a Young Women project involving homemaking skills applied to gospel principles. Each girl's banner declared before the public her private goal.

*NJO NJO NJO NJO NJO NJO NJO NJO NJO NJO*

It was an impressive sight, and the crowds cheered and applauded and gave them, at last, a standing ovation.

Earlier that afternoon a testimony meeting had followed the dress rehearsal. One after another, **not just ordinary** Young Men and Young Women stood and declared their gratitude for leaders who had worked together to stage this unforgettable, gigantic, and gorgeous dance festival for the youth of the multistake region. And they remembered the efforts of their own families and Church leaders, who had struggled to provide transportation through southern California traffic to countless rehearsals from widely scattered homes. These teenage dancers weepingly pledged to keep morally clean, be loyal to righteousness, defend the Church, and keep close to the Lord, whom they loved and intended to serve.

It was their finest hour and a happy one for me, for I was comforted that in the shade of gang wars, crime, and sexual gluttony in southern California, there was a saving remnant to help the Lord in his purposes.

## Near the Birthplace of the Prophet

In South Royalton, Vermont, near the birthplace of the Prophet Joseph Smith, a new chapel was dedicated. A meeting was then held for investigators, friends, neighbors, and the few members of the Church from miles around.

The Spirit was strong in the room. The music was mellow, and emotions ran high as a small youth group sang "Oh, How Lovely Was the Morning." Everyone gathered to learn more about the workings of God and the opportunities for personal growth in his church.

*NJO   NJO   NJO   NJO   NJO   NJO   NJO   NJO   NJO   NJO*

Following the dedicatory prayer, personal testimonies were shared. They were bold and inspiring. Most were given by people under twenty-five. Then the congregation divided into groups, and **not just ordinary** Young Men and Young Women assisted the full-time missionaries in explaining the gospel to their nonmember friends. It was awesome the way the Spirit flooded the hearts of good people. I watched the miracle of change happen as teenage boys and girls explained why their own lives were different because they were members of the Church. They committed themselves to Christ, and many baptisms resulted.

## From Utah to New England, Vancouver to Great Britain

For nearly twenty-five years the mountain states' *Deseret News* sponsored my "Seminar for Sallies and Sams"— a back-to-school event which became so popular that the productions were staged from Salt Lake to New England, from Vancouver to Great Britain, and many points in between, using local young men and young women who modeled their own clothing to show the latest young fashion trends. Each year was a different theme and script. There were panel discussions on how to make school terrific—everything from available scholarships to student activities—getting along with family and faculty, grooming tips, dating etiquette, making friends, and ideas for having fun together. There were guest appearances by famous people who demonstrated hairstyling, cooking, communication skills, problem-solving techniques, and community-service opportunities.

Thousands participated.

NJO NJO NJO NJO NJO NJO NJO NJO NJO NJO

Over the years I have followed the lives of many of the young people who have starred in or been a part of these programs in one way or another. One grew up to become the general president of the Relief Society; one is a General Authority. Many are Church workers, successful business people and community servants, translators for general conference, homemakers, and winners of major national awards. These were **not just ordinary** Young Men and Young Women. They have lived the standards of the Church, putting Christ in the core of their lives. They have worked hard and played fair.

They have proven that growing up wonderful prefaces growing old gracefully!

Following a seminar in London, England, a young girl and her friend approached me shyly. I looked into the shining eyes of one of Britain's best. "I want to be like they are," she said.

"They weren't like that at your age either!" I explained. "You'll get there if you keep it moving. Stay on the right path. Participate in Church activities. Call down the powers of heaven over you. Hang on to your ideals and your goals, no matter what."

I can still see her nodding her head vigorously, poking her elbow into her friend's side, and repeating, "I will. I am. I do!"

And it can happen to you.

## Southern Utah

The scene was the pioneer St. George Tabernacle. I stood on sacred ground as I spoke from the historic pulpit where prophecies had been uttered in early times—prophecies that had been fulfilled. The hall was filled to overflowing. The two-story-high windows

*NJO   NJO   NJO   NJO   NJO   NJO   NJO   NJO   NJO   NJO*

were open so people on the steps and lawn could hear. It was a special meeting sponsored by the Church Educational System. I was to encourage youth to find worthwhile, acceptable ways to have fun—assuring their growing up wonderful.

The choral number had changed my mood and influenced my talk. The choir had sung of loving one another—you know that song—and I thought of a pretty, faithful, **not just ordinary** Young Woman in faraway Europe. She was suffering from cancer—dying before she had really lived. I told them about her and casually suggested that perhaps one activity they could enjoy together would be to write letters of encouragement to her. I'd see that the stricken young woman got them.

I wondered if anyone was listening, but the days that followed proved that not only did they listen but they were moved to bring joy to someone who needed it. It was a miracle.

Letters, greeting cards, simple gifts, paperbacks, inspiring scripture in calligraphy, and so on arrived in a great show of the compassion of very alive-and-well young people. My desk was flooded! But so was her heart when the huge box of special greetings arrived from across the seas.

## Army Camp and Conversions

We were in a staff meeting for Church publications. The soldier was just back from military duty. He had joined the army right out of high school and left his little Mormon community as a real innocent, a high-principled person determined to keep God's commandments, no matter what!

NJO  NJO  NJO  NJO  NJO  NJO  NJO  NJO  NJO  NJO

He arrived at army camp, only to be assigned the bunk next to an older soldier who knew all the dirty words to say and said them, who knew all the wild things to do and did them. He kicked the youth kneeling in prayer at night. When alcoholic beverage was refused he forcefully pried open the Mormon's mouth to pour the liquor down his gullet. He spread pornographic pictures in the newcomer's bed so that when the young man turned back the bedding he couldn't avoid looking at them.

It was a miserable education for the farm boy with high ideals.

Then the troops went for overnight training on a cold plateau. The Mormon soldier had come prepared with two blankets. The hardened soldier had none. Temperatures dropped way down after midnight. The tough man lay there next to the kid and thought, "If this goody-goody were all that he pretends to be, he'd give me one of his blankets—I don't deserve it, but I need it."

And as the thought crossed his mind, the hand of the young boy handed over a blanket. And that did it. The next morning the older soldier awakened his companion early and said, "All right. Tell me what makes you this way. How could you give me your blanket after all the stuff you've taken from me? You should have put a knife in my back and twisted it after all I've put you through. What is it that makes you the way you are?"

And so the young man told him.

The life-changing gospel was taught. The hardened soldier became a member of the Church, and his personal growth began. He wrote to his brother stationed with the army somewhere else and told him to "find the Mormons because they are for real." The brother did that and was baptized. The two of them then sent many letters to their sister in mid-USA and told her about the Church. She joined. When the former tough soldier returned home he was a different person and soon became a leader of youth in his stake.

All because one Mormon boy believed in God, had the courage to live his religion, and dared to share it.

No wonder we say that among you are **not just ordinary** Young Men and Young Women! What a perspective I have gained from you! What a mark you are making on history!

## Greeks, Romans, and You

I often think of the perspective I received years ago from reading Ariel and Will Durant's *Story of Civilization.* As they state in their summational book *The Lessons of History*, they believe that known history shows little change in the conduct of mankind: "The Greeks of Plato's time behaved very much like the French of modern centuries; and the Romans behaved like the English. Means and instrumentalities change; motives and ends remain the same: to act or rest, to acquire or give, to fight or retreat, to seek association or privacy, to mate or reject, to offer or resent parental care."[2]

The Durants also conclude that there is little difference between classes as far as basic behavior goes. The same impulses stir both the rich and the poor. Other studies reveal that since the time of the Trojan War and the use of the Trojan horse, similar methods of disguise adopted by other rebels have been successful, whether in emerging countries or so-called civilized states. Custom and clothes change, but man's inner nature does not.

*NJO NJO NJO NJO NJO NJO NJO NJO NJO NJO*

Hamlet advised Polonius to treat the players "after [his] own honour and dignity" rather than their deserts.[3] Be your own master among your friends and acquaintances, you see, and being young—being alive at any age—won't be so difficult.

The invention of the wheel changed the world. Computers, with their systems of processing information, have changed the pace of life. What will never change is God's system and his principles—the laws irrevocably decreed in heaven before this earth was—established for man's fulfillment, success, and happiness. Morality, honesty, integrity, personal sacrifice, and love found in **not just ordinary** Young Men and Young Women and their older counterparts make the real difference.

Use your set of gifts in your own world. Try knocking off some of life's rough edges with all-out humor, or tilt others toward smiles through gentle persuasion. The details of a person's time line may vary; God's purposes and plan for his children on earth do not. Only this, his prophets have said that choice spirits have been reserved to come forth in these latter days.

And you have come!

You are **not just ordinary** Young Men and Young Women.

You are that generation prepared in premortal life to live on earth at this time of excitement and challenge. Think what it means to be born that much closer to the coming of Christ. You have a job to do, and it is about more than sharing chocolate so no one gets hurt, isn't it?

It's time now to pause in your life and celebrate being *you!*

*NJO  NJO  NJO  NJO  NJO  NJO  NJO  NJO  NJO  NJO*

# CHAPTER
## 2

# *Celebrate Yourself*

## Celebrate Yourself

So what's to celebrate? Check it out. Discover that there are some mighty fine things about being *you*. For instance:

1. Being born; having a crack at life; taking your turn on earth.
2. Being alive today!
3. Being a member of the Lord's "family," a member of his church, and having the blessings of leadership, programs, ordinances, and goals prescribed by him.
4. Knowing who you are, why you are here, and where you are going.
5. Counting your blessings—your talents, your particular trials, your family, the place you live, the people you know.
6. With all due respect to everybody else, to all the good and all the struggling souls on earth today—with *all* due respect—you recognize that it is awesome to be one of the young men and young women with a particular purpose.

There are some important things about being **not just ordinary** Young Men and Young Women. You see, you are part of a chosen generation. You were born at a certain time so that you could make a special contribution to mankind and play a key position on the Lord's team, if you will. You have been gathered together with a select group all across the world, fulfilling assignments given to you in the life before this one.

There is more.

You are like other out-of-the-ordinary Young Men and Young Women, yet you, yourself, are *unique* among them. You've discovered that being alike but being different offers some interesting challenges. So it will be a great day when you wake up to the reality that there is a system for coping with such challenges. You are on the Lord's side. You have your own heritage, your own hormones, your own gifts, your own childhood conditioning. You have your own particular problems. You have your very special cravings, yearnings, dreams, goals, and—ah, yes—shortcomings. But remember you also have your own testimony that you are a spirit child of Heavenly Father and are known to him. He knows more about you than even your earthly father to whom he assigned you! And both of them love you.

Is that great enough?

Okay, it is summary time. You are somewhat like everybody else on earth—living, breathing, functioning, loving, and getting ready to die someday. You also are like others in your special, chosen group of **not just ordinary** Young Men and Young Women in that you have a similar mission here on earth. You know things other teenagers don't—even the really nice ones. You have to be better than just nice. You have to try harder.

*NJO  NJO  NJO  NJO  NJO  NJO  NJO  NJO  NJO  NJO*

You are alike, but you are different. Your preparation for life will include distinguished dimensions.

For the most part, childhood was a piece of cake, wasn't it? Learning to walk, talk, manage toilet training, and then attend kindergarten was slick sledding. But then you stepped across the starting line to adolescence. This is life's most critical period. Now you are experiencing the crucial years, facing the crisis choices. And it's a big happening.

Once you've untied those apron strings and added "teen" after your age number, you learn a screaming fact: It is tough to live in the world but not be *of* it! But hang in there and read on! You'll soon find that there is value in being individual among your own generation—even individual among the rest of the **not just ordinary** Young Men and Young Women.

Your innocent view of goodness, peace, safety, easy-come-happiness turns into a mirage. You are assaulted with jarring obscenities, frustrated personalities taking their gripes out on you. The War between Good and Evil is under way and makes anything going on between nations seem like something out of an old movie. Some of the stuff you learned as a little kid is up for wondering. Life is not fair! All people don't seem to be created equal. Happiness isn't automatic just because you don't smoke or drink. God doesn't touch you with a magic wand on each shoulder to secure your secret desires just because you said your prayers last night. Sinners seem to be having all the fun. Parents have become people you don't know anymore. Nobody understands you, including yourself.

There you are, moving out of childhood with a beautiful burden on your back. You are supposed to grow up wonderful and do your thing. Well, for starters, remember that though you are in a particularly

NJO  NJO  NJO  NJO  NJO  NJO  NJO  NJO  NJO  NJO

appointed group, you—*you*—are in a class by yourself.

How do you cope with being chosen and being young, with being "not just ordinary" and yet anxious to be *like* and be *liked* by all your friends? You cope by doing good and avoiding evil no matter what! Remember, you can't fool with evil and feel good.

You cope by using your wits, by thinking first and acting afterwards, by continuing to learn truth—getting information to act upon—and by finding out what your specific purpose in life is. But above all, you work at keeping close to Heavenly Father.

For nearly six thousand years God held *you* in reserve to make your appearance in the final days before the Savior comes again to rule and reign on earth. You were born that much closer to that exciting time— later than your parents, your teachers, or the prophets on earth today. The First Presidency has stated: "You are not just ordinary young men and women. You are choice spirits who have been held in reserve to come forth in this day when the temptations, responsibilities, and opportunities are the very greatest."[4]

Do you know that every other generation before yours has drifted into apostasy? President Ezra Taft Benson has taught that ours will not because God has saved for the final inning some of his strongest spirit children, who will help bear off the kingdom triumphantly! "You are a marked generation," President Benson told a group of seminary and institute students in 1987. "There has never been more expected of the faithful in such a short period of time than there is of us. . . . The final outcome is certain—the forces of righteousness will finally win. But what remains to be seen is *where* each of us personally, now and in the future, will stand in this battle—and how tall will we stand?"[5]

*NJO   NJO   NJO   NJO   NJO   NJO   NJO   NJO   NJO   NJO*

William Wordsworth's words are worth a great deal when you consider the good counsel in his poem, "Character of the Happy Warrior." You see, you are warriors in the battle between good and evil, so find happiness in being, as Wordsworth wrote,

> More skilful in self-knowledge, even more pure,
> As tempted more; more able to endure,
> As more exposed to suffering and distress;
> Thence, also, more alive to tenderness.[6]

And Emily Dickinson wrote a passionate promise that you should memorize as a good reminder in dismal times:

> If I can stop one heart from breaking,
> I shall not live in vain;
> If I can ease one life the aching,
> Or cool one pain,
> Or help one fainting robin
> Unto his nest again,
> I shall not live in vain.[7]

In the booklet *For the Strength of Youth*, a special publication issued by the Church for youth, is the strong plea from the First Presidency of the Church, "We pray that you—the young and rising generation—will keep your bodies and minds clean, free from the contaminations of the world, that you will be fit and pure vessels to bear triumphantly the responsibilities of the kingdom of God in preparation for the second coming of our Savior."[8]

Now, we all agree that you are **not just ordinary** Young Men and Young Women. Bonded together in your respective organizations of Young Men and

*NJO  NJO  NJO  NJO  NJO  NJO  NJO  NJO  NJO  NJO*

Young Women, you can stand against the conniving, serious mischief makers walking Satan's path. Legs akimbo and arms locked, you are an awesome phalanx.

Standing tall against evil, you are an impressive group.

Individually how are you doing? Do you know how to be a man among men? Can you qualify as the girl of his dreams?

Read on . . .

# CHAPTER
## 3

*A Man
Among Men*

*and*

*A Pearl
of a Girl*

## A Man Among Men

Flex those muscles!
Boost your biceps!
Buy a disposable razor and keep it close by; you are about to become Mr. Wonderful, a man among men.

Until then, chalk up a list of qualities you are thankful to have. You'll see that you are already pretty great stuff—your bright eyes, windows to a brave and true soul; your eyelashes, long enough to make an innocent girl swoon; your body, coming right along; your story line, hilarious. You could be a stand-up comic. You've practiced clever lines and remembered to use them a lot of the time. Not always, but enough! After all, you don't want the other guys to hate you.

Your skills are developing. The appealing options for a life's work are narrowing. You are learning to match yourself with yourself, as a marathon runner does with his mile time.

You can't always control what happens to your voice in this time of change, but you can your life. You have learned how to walk cool, and you have no more doubt about what you will and won't go along with.

*NJO   NJO   NJO   NJO   NJO   NJO   NJO   NJO   NJO   NJO*

# A Pearl of a Girl

Once upon a happy time ago, you were born a daughter. You awakened each day smiling through your yawns. Mother was there, approving of you. Daddy was there, loving you. You were his girl.

God was in his heaven, and all was right in your world.

Then you began to grow. You went from a squishy-legged, dimpled darling to the tooth fairy's best friend. You shifted from "Mother's little helper" to "Mother's pain in the neck" because you borrowed her things, you monopolized the phone, you had homework that could be done only during the dinner hour, and your hair never "worked."

Daddy didn't understand you at all. You had traded sitting on his lap for spending time with *that* boy, and Daddy hoped you didn't sit on *that* lap! And you sulked a lot.

You couldn't understand yourself, for a lot of years. Daddy called you "Princess" and you felt like one (except when your hair didn't "work," which was much of the time). In front of your own bedroom mirror you

# A Man Among Men

You can be in the world—work, play, study, cavort—but your life, your way, your goals, your systems for positive results are in place. Hands on your head at eight. Hands on your head at twelve and fourteen and sixteen, and looking ahead to later ordinations. That makes all the difference to you. Let others waste away life if they choose, pretend they are a can of worms instead of a priesthood holder, but that's not for you. You prepared for these occasions. Like a young Joseph or a Daniel, you pray in a private place. God is there for you, and you like that feeling of being on his errand. You want to know for yourself about important things that have roots in today. This time of your young manhood is the solid rock upon which all the rest of your foreverness is built. And it's good.

You pay close attention to how the leadership at church conducts the meetings, handles the kids graduating from Primary and the girls getting their awards. You listen to the prayers and the blessings in a priesthood circle. You're getting it down about praying to God the Father in the name of Jesus Christ. No mixed metaphors and wrong salutations for you. And what's this about "unrighteous dominion"? No way. You agree that it is not the answer to happiness at home or in the priesthood quorum or with girls. So long, chauvinism, and hello, great guy and good leader on whatever level.

You want to be "chosen," and you know that you do. Admit it! Remember that many are called but few are chosen, and that's because many have their hearts set upon the things of this world. Some men aspire to the honors of men. But you are learning how real disciples of Christ who hold the priesthood of God function and what their goals are. Recite and apply words

*NJO  NJO  NJO  NJO  NJO  NJO  NJO  NJO  NJO  NJO*

# A Pearl of a Girl

had real possibilities—which quickly vanished on your way to school.

How to win control of yourself? How to be what you want to be? How to know what you want to be? How to make your hair "work"?

How to be a pearl of a girl? A pearl of a girl all the way up the age ladder, too.

For starters, you begin where you are, use what you have to work with, and move steadily in the direction of your field of dreams. You expect delightful surprises.

Get organized. Make lists. Set goals. Sort and sift and select on the basis of *your* life. Recite: "To every thing there is a season. . . ." Check it out in Ecclesiastes 3—that scripture says it all, doesn't it?

You make value judgments all along the way, learning what to take hold of and what to cast aside. When to control and when to submit. When to steal the scene and when to boost the ego of someone else.

You have your belief system programmed in. You benefit by the positives—you are a child of God, your life has a purpose, there is a "Super Plan," and someone watches over you and wants you to make it. Your life tests will be different from someone else's. So will your strengths. (Every tennis match ends in 6–0, 6–0 for the other player? At least you don't trip yourself up at the game of life.)

No way, absolutely no way, will you allow yourself to hang out in the dark corners of negativism. Catch yourself in *that* act and you'll stomp on the statements like "I can't," "I'm afraid," "It's too hard," "I'm not good enough." Shout out, "I can try!"

And you keep on growing. You keep pace with what is happening with programs for **not just ordinary**

*NJO NJO NJO NJO NJO NJO NJO NJO NJO NJO*

# A Man Among Men

like *gentleness, meekness,* and *love unfeigned.* A man among men works his wonders through persuasion and without hypocrisy or guile. There is hardly a woman of any age who doesn't love to see grown men cry. A strong boy or man with a tender, caring heart is some kind of wonderful!

Imagine, your rights as a priesthood bearer are inseparably connected with the powers of heaven! It's like *wow!* That's why real heavenly service happens only upon the principle of righteousness. You are getting good at that, all right. Biceps are one thing, but a steel spine and a solid soul make you a man among men of whatever size.

You like your gang—the lunchtime crowd, the team, the quorum members. All right, so you envy the bigger athletes you know. But a cheering section is as vital to the game as the running back—almost! You marvel at someone else's cool around girls. Never mind, your day will come. First a mission, safe and sound and unencumbered.

You have figured out that if you want friends you have to be one. You find a way to get laughs or feel confidence without sarcasm or bullying. Since it didn't come naturally you read up on being a people pleaser instead of a problem person. You've worked it out with Dad to take a group of you fishing. Ah, snowmobiling? To see the pro ball game?

You wish Dad would remember how it was and understand how you have to be, but you figure on working all that out in time. Why, you can do anything—except press your Sunday shirt wrinkle-free and keep the troublesome zits off your cheeks.

You are getting better. You can talk straight, say what you mean and mean what you say. Sure, it has

*NJO NJO NJO NJO NJO NJO NJO NJO NJO NJO*

# A Pearl of a Girl

Young Women. You keep matching your disappointments against your successes.

You study and pray and experiment on the word to increase your faith. Faith is at your core. The Light of Christ is the center of your being.

You stand for truth and goodness, fairness and free agency for all people.

You begin to understand how great is the worth of the human soul.

You witness the inevitability of sowing and harvesting, cause and effect, choices and accountability.

You have a life and you can change. You have a mission and you can be constant. Your feet are on the ground but your reach is for heaven.

And you love, love, love Mom and Dad and the siblings; the dear old man on a walker down the block; the YW leader who coaxes you through the system; the tutor for your college exams; and Heavenly Father, who hears and answers your prayers, whose Spirit quickens yours.

Now, listen to a prophet's voice: "I hope our young women of the Church will establish early in their lives a habit of Christian service. When we help other people with their problems, it puts ours in fresh perspective. We encourage the sisters of the Church—young and older—to be 'anxiously engaged' in quiet acts of service for friends and neighbors."[9]

The way to become a pearl of a girl is to remember who you really are. Keep yourself clean inside and out. Keep yourself healthy, and work to be wise—learn God's lessons.

Fix yourself up pretty as can be, shining from crown to soles. Modulate your voice to match your facial expression. Your face, you know, reveals what is

*NJO  NJO  NJO  NJO  NJO  NJO  NJO  NJO  NJO  NJO*

# A Man Among Men

taken a lot of private practice—rehearsals before the date or the sacrament prayer or the job interview.

Speaking of speaking, *no* was probably your first word. Hopefully your last one won't be one of the ugly uglies—a four-letter obscenity. Mercy! And may you never, never take God's name in vain, as the anti-Christ and the godless makers of movies do. That commandment still applies in this day if you want to be a man among men. As for being a gentleman among girls, try helping them see the foolishness of their unappealing ways if they swear.

The hands that pass the sacrament, baptize a child, or hold a girl's ought to be clean. The day you invested in your own set of finger tools—cuticle snippers, nail file, orange stick, and a bottle of cuticle remover—was a move to last all the rest of your life. You'll be glad you made it. Car repairing, gas pumping, forking the fertilizer, or scrimmaging notwithstanding, there is no excuse today for the black scourge among knuckles and nails.

And listen, the sooner you believe the new news about sex, the better your decision making will be. And your frustrations will be under control. You may need to take more cooling showers or throw more basketballs if your chemistry suddenly seems compatible with cute li'l what's-her-name. But the hokum about hormones that the world preaches has no place in your belief system. You've checked it over. You believe in God and in his goodness in making the rules for real happiness. You know—yeah, you know—hormones can ruin you if you pay too much attention to body stuff. It's your spirit that never dies, you believe. And right you are. So you go by the spiritual promptings, not the R-rated material. You know that God gives no

*NJO   NJO   NJO   NJO   NJO   NJO   NJO   NJO   NJO   NJO*

# A Pearl of a Girl

inside you—nice, naughty, or vain. And the face you have when you are forty is exactly what you deserve, I've always said. (Oh yes, you'll grow up to at least turn forty—hopefully!)

Eat well, sleep only enough, hustle your homework, and help with the housework. Get good ideas for good times. Train your ears to hear, your eyes to truly see, and your heart to pound with caring.

Be glad you are you, not another instead. It isn't how tall or how small you turn out to be; it's what you are inside that counts.

Girls, as women yours is the gift to love, to influence for good. Get those young men to go on missions. Insist on clean language and topics of conversation from them, so that they are as careful to avoid swearing and gossiping as you are. (You are, aren't you?) Your gift of love should extend to older people, and to the little folks you tend. It should extend to teachers at church and parents at home. Find appropriate ways to be kind to all who cross your path. I know a group of young women who all decided to wear striped t-shirts on the same day to school. They got the word around to all the girls in their crowd—except one, who was not absolutely, killingly cute and popular! Their trick worked, of course. Yes, she was crushed, felt out of it, cried at home, and hated to go back to school the next day. How would you feel!

Think before you break a heart—even halfway.

## You'll Want to Remember . . .

You have megabytes to burn. Think about this idea: Imagine a great factory where little or no work is

# A Man Among Men

commandment unless he knows it can be kept, that he gives them for the good of man—and for you and your girlfriend, too. It's called hands off.

Some people never get over the flexing-muscle stage. Thank God you are heart and soul, head and shoulders above the rest. You are, in fact, at whatever age and stage, a Mr. Wonderful, a **not just ordinary** Young Man!

## You'll Want to Remember . . .

You have megabytes to burn. Think about this idea: Imagine a great factory where little or no work is done: buildings that cover acres, miles on miles of corridors, rooms after rooms, machines of a hundred different kinds. Every known scientific device, every known scientific principle in usable form is embodied in one room or another, there is equipment more perfect than anything ever before dreamed of. But that whole great plant, with all its possibilities, all its intricate mechanism, is standing idle, not abandoned, but not kept up. Only the footfalls of watchmen echo along the empty corridors; cobwebs are across the windows, around the doorknobs, between the spokes of the great flywheels, and thick dust over everything. The delicately adjusted machinery is motionless, rusting silently away; the whole wonderful plant, with all its marvelous equipment, practically going to waste.

What is it?

That's a leading psychologist's idea of the average human mind. But since you are anything but average, start burning those megabytes in the program of the Lord to move you toward your highest possibility.

# A Pearl of a Girl

done: buildings that cover acres, miles on miles of corridors, rooms after rooms, machines of a hundred different kinds. Every known scientific device, every known scientific principle in usable form is embodied in one room or another, there is equipment more perfect than anything ever before dreamed of. But that whole great plant, with all its possibilities, all its intricate mechanism, is standing idle, not abandoned, but not kept up. Only the footfalls of watchmen echo along the empty corridors; cobwebs are across the windows, around the doorknobs, between the spokes of the great flywheels, and thick dust over everything. The delicately adjusted machinery is motionless, rusting silently away; the whole wonderful plant, with all its marvelous equipment, practically going to waste.

What is it?

That's a leading psychologist's idea of the average human mind. But since you are anything but average, start burning those megabytes in the program of the Lord to move you toward your highest possibility.

# CHAPTER

## 4

# *Your Future Has a Past*

# Your Future Has a Past

Angie hefted all her luggage from the transport bus. It was here at the airport that the dawn came up like thunder, not in Mandalay, as the boys' choir had sung at graduation.

*Graduation from high school. Now on to real life,* Angie mused. Graduation just three days over and today was the first day of the rest of her life—she was off and away to find out who she *really* was.

Only 7:00 A.M. and there was no morning stillness—buses chugging, gears grinding, horns blasting and whistles sounding, speaker systems droning flight information, the call of cabbies, and skycaps shouting. All this confusion didn't help Angie's fluttering stomach.

That, and no sign of Chad.

Angie looked back at the bus, watching the driver roll the destination sign from Airport to Poplar Grove. It would be heading back to her community, her bus stop, her home. Home? She half turned to reboard the bus and go back. It was tempting. She'd never known any other home than Poplar Grove. Maybe she *was* making a mistake to use her graduation money for this trip. Her weeping parents thought so. Still, it was her life and she had made her decision. Angie's heart pounded and her mouth felt dry as she resolutely turned her back on the bus. She brushed the back of her flawless hand across the moisture on her forehead and looked again for Chad.

Where was he? He'd promised to be there to say good-bye.

Probably he overslept.

Probably he didn't recall what an important trip this was for her.

Probably he didn't care! Boys!

She looked up and down the area. No sign of him. She checked her watch again and admitted she was a few minutes early. There was still time for Chad to make it.

Angie nervously smoothed the sleeve of her Laura Ashley print blouse, suddenly conscious of her own firm, young flesh and bone beneath it. Good health from all those dancing raisins she'd eaten for breakfast while riding to the airport! As Chad always said, "I don't eat anything unless I see it dancing and singing on TV." She smiled at this small effort toward courage. Again she searched the walkways for Chad.

At last he appeared, quite a distance down the platform, but jogging his way toward gate 12. *Yes, that's Chad,* she thought, *wearing acid-dyed jeans and, in spite of the warm weather, his letter jacket earned in track.* She watched him as he effortlessly dodged people and leaped over stacked luggage and packages, skitted around push carts, danced past unloading

*NJO  NJO  NJO  NJO  NJO  NJO  NJO  NJO  NJO  NJC*

areas and car-rental transport vans, and slid into her arms.

Angie sighed. Everything would be all right now.

But would it really? Chad was still angry, as he had been graduation night. The hug that he gave her now turned into a shake. He took her by the shoulders and cried out, "Angie, why are you doing this? Have you lost it altogether, girl? Wow, you know how to ruin a guy's biggest summer."

"Chad, I'm so glad you are here. Only please, don't make it harder for me. You know I have to do this. We talked about it graduation night."

"Well, I still can't understand your thinking. What's wrong with *Here?*"

"I don't know yet because I haven't been *There!*"

Silence between them. Chad thrust his hands deep into his jeans pockets. Angie wrapped her arms about herself in a kind of holding pattern. They studied the terrazzo platform as if they were going to be graded on it.

Then Angie looked at Chad earnestly and said, "Chad, you don't understand why I have to do this, because you *know* who you are and I don't. I don't even know where this came from." She tugged at a lock of startling red hair that set her apart from other girls.

"You have never worried about this before. It's that letter your mom got. That's it. The letter!"

"Yes, it's the letter. But don't bug me about this, Chad, because for a long time, secretly, I have wondered who I really was. The letter came and now I have to follow up. I have to. But help me. I am frightened, you know."

"I'll do anything for you, Angie. But I don't want to lose you." Chad's fuzzy jawline tightened, and he looked away for a moment to ease his frustration. "You are leaving all you hold sacred to run off and find out where your crazy red hair came from?"

"Chad? Look at me—no, wait." There was one last hope to help him understand. She'd show him the letter. Angie unzipped the duffel bag and scavanged around a moment. Its contents spilled as she stirred up her yearbook, old photographs, a tutu from her childhood ballet recital, a plaster cast of her hand made in kindergarten . . .

Then she took out an envelope.

"Here's the infamous letter. Mom said I should keep it secret, but I think you need to read it. You are my best friend and I want you to understand. Here. Read it." She thrust it at him and he snatched it from her.

Soberly Chad read the words that could change both of their lives. Then he looked deep into Angie's eyes and said, "Hmm. Well. I see what you mean. I see why you want to go meet her. But you don't have to live with her! Remember she is really a total stranger."

He stuffed the letter back into the envelope and slapped it into Angie's hands.

"At least I'll know who I am," she said softly.

"I can tell you who you are. I can tell you more about you than this stranger can."

"Chad, this stranger is my mother!"

"*She* isn't your mother. Mrs. Clifford is your mother —that kindly, hardworking secretary to the principal at High—she's your mother. You've always lived with the Cliffords. Ah, come on, Angie, get with it."

Angie put the letter back in the duffel and then slowly turned her hand over, cupping the fingers into

*NJO NJO NJO NJO NJO NJO NJO NJO NJO NJO*

her palm. She studied them, carefully examining nails and knuckles, flexing the fingers, stretching them apart, touching the thumb to each one in miraculous movement. These slender, girlish fingers and callus-free hands could bring music from a violin, grasp a volleyball and send it spinning over the net, could guide a ballpoint or work cross-stitch with a fine needle.

"Yes," agreed Angie, "I have always lived with the Cliffords, and I love them." She pointed toward the duffel as she continued: "But *she* gave me these, Chad, not Mrs. Clifford. *She* is my birth mother. *She* gave me flesh and bone. *She* gave me this!" Angie tucked the long red hair behind her ears.

"So she gave you red hair. Well, Mrs. Clifford gave you her heart! She may not have given you genes and things, but she sure as crocodiles fed your incredibly beautiful growth. And I'll tell you another thing, Angeline Clifford, Mrs. Clifford taught you values and how to make smart choices. Graduation night as a case in point. Don't forget that."

Angie's half-smile and slight blush proved she was listening. Chad grabbed the advantage and looked at her, tenderly pleading.

"Angie, Angie, if you leave now I may never see you again."

"Oh, you'll see me again. You are right about Mother Clifford. I'll be back, Chad. Besides, how can I stay away from a good thinker like you?"

"Then why all this luggage for just an overnight visit?"

"Why, indeed?" agreed Angie. With that she turned to her pile of luggage. She picked up only the duffel and the box of candy her mother had tucked under her arm as a gift for her "hostess."

"Take the rest of this stuff home for me, will you, Chad? Please? See you soon." Angie swept by, kissing him on the cheek before running to gate 12.

## Who Are You?

You know your name, but do you know who else you are?

Who are the people who came before you?

Who gave you some of themselves?

Who left their mark? Whose nose do you have? Whose olive skin?

What do you know about the parents who gave you heart?

Get to know the people who went before you in your family line and you'll know more about yourself. And someday part of what you are you will pass on to your own children and then to their children and their children . . . whew! Now that's how your past has a future.

## Finding Out Who You Are

Have yourself a fascinating time making a family record. Below you will find some steps for gathering information, as well as instructions on how to make your own pedigree chart and organize the information about your past—your beginnings—so that everything will be ready for those who will one day be in your future.

Making a pedigree chart is another way of saying "draw your family tree." You'll probably be able to locate a commercially prepared pedigree chart that allows you to merely fill in the blanks. Included here is a picture of a chart, and following are directions regarding how to make one of your own:

1. Take a sheet of type paper and turn it sideways.

2. Draw a two-inch line in the middle of the paper but close to the left edge. Make it go side to side or parallel to the top of the page.

3. Draw steps of lines as shown in the accompanying illustration.

4. Put your full name on the first line. Put your father's full name on the first line of the upper steps. Put your mother's full name on the first line of the lower steps (be sure to include her maiden name, the name she had before she got married).

5. Now you are ready to find out what names go on the other steps. You'll need to ask your mother for the names of her parents and of their parents, as far back as she can go. You will need to ask your father the same questions. You can look in the yellow pages of your phone book under "Genealogy" and get directed to your local archives or genealogical library. If you have the name of a grandparent or another ancestor, you can get started tracing your family history in the records of the archives or historical records library.

Once you've started this project it will be hard to stop working on your family record. You'll want pictures. You'll probably want details such as birthdays and wedding dates and death records. Even home addresses would be interesting to include—at least cities and states.

A fine thing will probably happen to you as you work at this. You'll feel as if you are beginning to know your ancestors. You'll even start thinking about what kind of posterity you might have. You'll surely know more about yourself than just your name. And you'll understand the wonderful truth that your very own future has a past.

*NJO NJO NJO NJO NJO NJO NJO NJO NJO NJO*

# PEDIGREE CHART

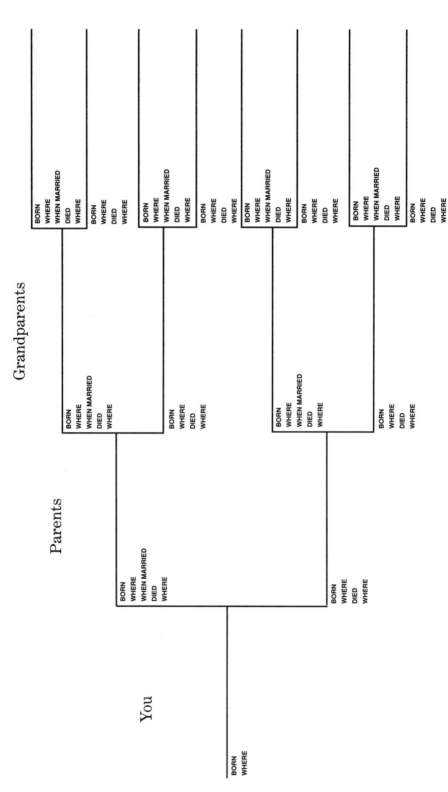

You

Parents

Grandparents

Great-grandparents

BORN
WHERE

BORN
WHERE
WHEN MARRIED
DIED
WHERE

BORN
WHERE
DIED
WHERE

BORN
WHERE
WHEN MARRIED
DIED
WHERE

BORN
WHERE
DIED
WHERE

BORN
WHERE
WHEN MARRIED
DIED
WHERE

BORN
WHERE
DIED
WHERE

BORN
WHERE
WHEN MARRIED
DIED
WHERE

BORN
WHERE
DIED
WHERE

BORN
WHERE
WHEN MARRIED
DIED
WHERE

BORN
WHERE
DIED
WHERE

BORN
WHERE
WHEN MARRIED
DIED
WHERE

BORN
WHERE
DIED
WHERE

BORN
WHERE
WHEN MARRIED
DIED
WHERE

BORN
WHERE
DIED
WHERE

## Special Circumstances

Were you adopted?

Being adopted has its blessings. You were chosen. You also were prayed for and anxiously awaited. Every wonderful unfolding of your physical, mental, and spiritual being was a delightful surprise to your grateful parents. They would do anything for you—and no doubt *did* along the way.

Being adopted also has its problems. Most adopted people know very little of their medical history, for example. There is usually scant information available regarding genes from long-gone ancestors that contribute to your being.

For your information only, when a child is adopted into an active LDS family who want the child sealed to them by the power of the priesthood in a temple of God, this can only be done when the legal requirements have been met. For example, in some states, after six months, the adoptive parents finalize the adoption proceedings in a court of law. Other states and countries have different restrictions. The temple sealing can only happen after the legal work is done. Then in the sacred ceremony in the house of the Lord, the child is sealed to the adoptive father and mother and they become a family for all eternity as though it had happened naturally in the beginning.

In collecting family history and filling in the blanks on a genealogical pedigree chart, the adopted child follows the genealogical line of his or her adoptive parents. If the time comes when information is found about the natural or birth parents, that information can be recorded as well on separate sheets.

The gathering of families in an orderly manner is a vital part of Heavenly Father's plan for us. Adopted or not, we are all Heavenly Father's children. We have ancestors and hopefully will have a posterity. We keep records so that no one is lost or forgotten to us, and so that we will understand ourselves better. God will never forget us, of course, because we belong to him. However, he wants us to know our ancestors. Keeping our own record will help those who come after us.

## About Your Own Gathering

Make a vow now to record whatever information you can gather about your beginnings—ancestors, national heritage, family gifts and traits. Maybe you are devoted readers or into music or lovers of nature. Add what you know about yourself—the *you* that you are today. Somebody sometime will be glad for the perspective.

If you keep a journal or diary, your own offspring will have an easier time of knowing their roots and the influences that modify them.

There are many kinds of materials that speak of a person's life. There are many methods of gathering them together in an orderly fashion. There are genealogical-line records. There are personal journals or diaries, kept currently as your life moves along. There are life-story records in which you write about what has happened to you, the people in your circle of family and friends, the places you have lived, the Church service you've given, the experiences of school and work, the talents you've developed. And especially you record the way your life has been blessed by Heavenly Father—the miracles and answers to prayer, the guidance and protection you have received from the Lord through the power of the Holy Ghost.

*NJO  NJO  NJO  NJO  NJO  NJO  NJO  NJO  NJO  NJO  NJC*

One of the rare thrills of my life was to handle a personal journal written by the Prophet Joseph Smith. Written in the front of this journal are these words: "Joseph Smith, Jr.'s Book for Record Baught on the 27th of November 1832 for the purpose to keep a minute account of all things that come under my observation &c."

The first line of his first entry in the diary reads, "Oh may God grant that I may be directed in all my thaughts. Oh bless thy servent. Amen." His first words were a prayer—how touching! Nephi wrote the first words that appear in the Book of Mormon: "I, Nephi, having been born of goodly parents . . ."

What will your first words be in your new personal record book? What will your posterity learn about you just by what you record?

A portion of President Spencer W. Kimball's personal history has a first line that lures the reader into the rest of the writing. He is a poet as well as a prophet, as we learn by reading his entry:

"This is a record of one silent, sleepless night which I spent in 1957 in a bedroom on the third floor of the Mission Home in New York City following major surgery in which I lost one vocal cord and part of another and then had staph infection following the surgery.

"For all the long hours of the seemingly endless night I suffered and reminisced."[10]

This record is a beautiful retreat from bitter pain. It also introduces another writing style for the personal record keeper, a wonderful weaving of a current experience with recollections from childhood. The following excerpt from President Kimball's personal record shows what a workable format this is:

"The night is wearing on. The New Yorkers about

NJO  NJO  NJO  NJO  NJO  NJO  NJO  NJO  NJO  NJO

us on Park and Fifth Avenues in their tuxedos and evening dresses are still early in their evening's festivities.

"I am wandering again, back to childhood. We are at a picnic, all the good Thatcher folks. We have come on horseback, in buggies and in wagons to old Cluff's ranch. We enjoy the great swings from the monumental cottonwoods. There is lemonade for sale. The picnic dinner is incomparable.

"The swim in the pond is the ultimate—everybody goes in swimming. No skimpy bathing suits here—people are wearing dresses, stockings, and overalls. Father is such a good swimmer. How I wish I could swim as he does! All over the great pond he moves easily and seemingly without effort. Now he comes for me, his little boy. I am on his back with my arms around his neck so tightly that he must constantly warn me. The water is deep and I am scared, and I plead with him to take me back to the shallow water. At last we feel ground, and I say, 'I'm all right now, Pa,' and I see him turn and swim off toward deep water. I start toward shore and step into a deep hole. Down, down, down! Water is filling my lungs. . . . I cannot scream! Why doesn't someone get help? Will they never rescue me? Someone has now seen my predicament. Pa has heard their screams and is after me. I am full of water and coughing, spitting, crying for a long time. I thought I was drowned.

"But how did I get way down to Arizona again? O yes, I heard the whistle of a boat on the East River, which reminded me of the youngsters swimming in it and diving from the scraggy rocks. We saw them last week as we took the Circle trip around Manhattan Island. How I wish I could swim like those little urchins! If I could have swum like that when I was a child—and

*NJO NJO NJO NJO NJO NJO NJO NJO NJO NJO*

then my mind had relived the near-drowning experience in Arizona."[11]

As you make your entries in your own record book, be sure to put the day of the week and the complete date. Time of day is a nice addition, too, as is location. Are you home or on a trip? away at school? on a mission? Name the location if it is other than your home address, which ought to be listed in your record book someplace already.

Professional historians urge that records be kept on a high quality, acid-free paper, and that legal black ink or print ribbon be used.

A life recorded is a life twice lived. You live your life the best you can. You obey God's command to record it. You enjoy the permanence of your memories. We all say, "I'll never forget. . . ." But before we know it we have forgotten some important thought, event, lesson, or details of a precious relationship.

In John 1:22 we read, "What sayest thou of thyself?" Remember, your future has a past.

Now that your future has a past, what is ahead? What are the good moves to make and the senseless sins to avoid to make it all—for sure—turn out great?

*NJO NJO NJO NJO NJO NJO NJO NJO NJO NJO*

# CHAPTER
## 5

# *Give Me Five!*

# Give Me Five!

## Five Senseless Sins

" 'For all that, let me tell you, brother Panza,' said Don Quixote, 'that there is no recollection to which time does not put an end, and no pain which death does not remove.'

" 'And what greater misfortune can there be,' replied Panza, 'than one that must wait for time to end it and death to remove it?' "[12]

In other words, your worst mistakes, your wildest nightmares won't disappear with the dawn. Better to avoid such trouble in the first place.

Here are five foolish mistakes, five stupid moves, five senseless sins that can ruin your life, as well as your sleep.

1. *Believing that everybody is doing it.* It's a fact that everybody is *not* doing it. You aren't, for example. Of course, the worldly-minded will attempt to get you off your pedestal to "do it"—whatever "it" is. It can be the beginning of trouble for you if you heed the howl of

the witless herd and give in. Even if it seems that a lot of people are doing something that is physically, mentally, legally, or spiritually abusive, you had better stay away from such decisions. Numbers have never made a wrong right. Stupid sin, which amounts to self-destruction, is not for you.

2. *Assuming that your generation invented sex, drugs, and speed on the highway.* Can you hear the familiar cry? "But things are different now!" No, they are not that different. Adam and Eve knew about sex before you were thought of. Cain killed Abel not too many years into man's recorded history. People have always had the same temptations that you have today (they come under different labels now, that's all), and you have the same commandments that other people have had throughout the generations.

3. *Forgetting who you are.* You are not like everybody else. You have walked in holy places. You have had hands placed upon your head for blessings from God. You may forget a lot of things—your mother's birthday or your Social Security number—but don't forget who you are and what your goals are. All eternity is at stake. Would you be so foolish as to plan on a university education and then go ahead and crash your grades in high school?

4. *Lying to your bishop.* Never lie to your bishop. You can't get away with it in the long haul. He's inspired and called by God to watch over the people of your ward. The Holy Ghost lets him know if you are telling the truth or not. Don't lie to your parents, either. That goes hand in hand with the mistaken notion that grown-ups don't understand or can't remember or should mind their own business. It is far better to work at avoiding sin than to multiply ways of covering it up.

*NJO NJO NJO NJO NJO NJO NJO NJO NJO NJO*

5. *Refusing to recognize truth.* Ignoring the symptoms. Passing over the fruits of obedience. Going the way of the world. Refusing counsel. Dishonoring your parents. Quitting the business of personal prayer. Blowing your one chance to live. This is heavy stuff here. Watch yourself. Be honest with yourself. Keep in mind the idea that even bank robberies are spawned in someone who probably started with doing something like stealing pennies.

## Five Good Moves

It has been said, "The evil that men do lives after them."[13] On the other hand, it can also be said the good that men do lives after them. Try that out in life! Jesus lived two thousand years ago in a remote corner of the earth—but what a following! To become like the Savior a person has to do more than slap somebody's palm!

Here are five good moves, five shining moments, five wonderful ways to make life better.

1. *Improve the shining moments.* One chance to live, and it is the season to be young. Make every moment better than you expected—like the times with your friends, the talks with your parents, the performance with your musical group, the meetings at youth conference, the wonder of winning a game, the gratitude for a prayer answered. Improving and reaching should be beyond your grasp—"else what's a heaven for?" asked the poet. A moment becomes shining when you perform beyond your natural ability—just as if you were God-blessed!

2. *Thank God you are blessed.* You are **not just** an **ordinary** Young Man or Young Woman; you are God-blessed. If ever an identity crisis occurs in your life or

your self-worth sags, claim your blessings. Ask and it *shall* be given . . . you! You may have to work through some tough times, rotten relationships, ugly temptations, searing sicknesses, but you will be blessed with strength to endure, to overcome, to find joy. And that's the truth. Repeat after me, and then twenty times more, "I am loved—no matter what, God loves me." Then feel the healing happen.

3. *Keep growing in the gospel.* Someone once said something like, "A lot of people are just religious enough to be miserable: they can't be happy at a wild party, and they feel uncomfortable at testimony meeting." But not you. The more you learn through precept and prayer about the gospel and God, the more comfortable you feel on your knees, in the chapel, in the midst of the world. It's a shining moment indeed when you feel the grace of God wrap around you like a fleece blanket. With God, nothing is impossible.

4. *Dream a great dream.* Make your part of the world a kinder, gentler place. Dream a great dream of being a people pleaser instead of a problem person. You can do things nobody else can do. You might be the one to strive for the Olympic gold and set a brave example by comforting the losers. You might be the one to wheel your mom around and be her legs for errands. You might be the one to make friends with a new foreign student at school who is laughed at. One such girl had an ice-cream cone thrown in her locker at school by guys who stood by waiting for the chance. A younger student put her arm around the girl, offered to help her clean up the mess and to walk home from school with her. Let your enthusiasm (which means something like "God in you") show. It's contagious.

5. *Learn.* Learn how to say no and make it stick. Learn from the mistakes of others, such as people in

the scripture stories, celebrity press, family members, and friends. When you and your mom were the world, she told you about burning your fingers on hot stoves, didn't she? Learn from what those in authority over you *now* have to teach. Learn what is truth and what is trend. Learn which truths are critical (it is true that an egg cooks in boiled water, but that's not as important as knowing the true reason behind chastity). Learn which trends are fun and which are cheapening or even dangerous.

When you plant a tree, you will remove about twenty-five pounds of carbon dioxide from the air every year. Too much carbon dioxide is a culprit, so you are an environmental helper. When you plant a seed in someone's heart that you know that Jesus lives, loves us, and has a plan that works for the happy life—when you plant *that* seed, you've changed people.

## You'll Want to Remember . . .

To wrap up this information in the corner of your brain, think of "Give me five!" Five senseless sins and five good moves spelled out for you. Try making your own list of the good and not-so-good points that positively or negatively can affect your happiness, your holiness, your opportunities for success and the realization of your personal potential.

You were reared in a certain family, and that has an impact on your life, too. Better take another look at family life and find its value. Heavenly Father didn't command us to honor father and mother without good reason.

# CHAPTER
## 6

*Yo, Dad!*
*Oh, Mom!*

## Yo, Dad! Oh, Mom!

A family is God's way of blessing the world.

A family keeps a mother from doing all the things she's always wanted to do until she is too old to do them. But somewhere along the way a family weaves such magic that one day Mother realizes that this, after all, *is* what she wanted to do all along. As for fathers, they have to shave every day.

A family is full of people helping people. Bigger people help little ones, and the middle group play it both ways.

Families, always multiplied by two, come in a wide range of mathematical combinations. This unique variety pack offers assorted sizes, shapes, colors, temperaments, creeds, heritages, dwelling places, and bank accounts. Each additional member to any family unit challenges, for a time, the lofty premise that all men are created equal, because that newcomer gets far more attention per hour than everyone else put together.

And it is okay.

## The Roles of Different Family Members

As we study the individual components it is easy to see what makes families exactly the way they are, generation after generation. From the youngest to the oldest, each member has a part to play.

The youngest member of the family is termed "baby." This has nothing to do with age. Actually it is rather a state of being, for whether six months or sixty years, the last born is persistently and lovingly referred to as "the baby."

Babies are for picking—picking at, picking up, and picking up after. Babies are also for kissing and caring, bedding and bottling, holding and hugging, diapering and doing a thousand other things to restore peace. Babies come equipped with an amazing gift for melting the most macho father into a reasonable facsimile of jelly. They convince a mother that she'd rather have her hands in detergent than suntan lotion any day. Babies offer the only reasonable explanation for lisping when you are hovering precariously past middle age.

Babies cause parents to love each other more deeply, to smile more through tears, to buy more film, to lose more sleep, to stay home more, and to become more boring. But they also remind them that heaven is really very close after all.

You see, babies are for loving.

The next age-group in the family is referred to as the "terrible twos toddlers." These little destroying angels may be found wherever there is water. They are also known to slide down the best furniture, sneeze when spoon-fed, and move restlessly from room to room, leaving their trail behind them. The only time "terrible twos toddlers" are quiet is when they are doing something they shouldn't. They have a disarming way of charming, smiling their sweetest smile when they are about to be disciplined.

Toddlers are on the threshold of a great new world of learning. Toddlers are for teaching—teaching to sing, to pray, to read, to tie shoes, to eat with forks instead of fingers, to understand that training pants are the road to freedom. One of the nice things about a toddler is that he loves you unabashedly, anyway.

Oh, toddlers are for loving.

The next group is the grade-school gang. Grade-schoolers are famous for giggles and gum, the blank spaces in the front of their smiles, freckles sprinkled generously across the bridge of the nose, and for telling family secrets to neighbors.

Grade-schoolers have a talent for running—running noses, running away, running errands, running the bathroom water the longest with the least to show for it.

They are for getting—getting measles at Christmas, and getting into trouble when you aren't looking. They are skilled at getting things into drawers already too full of stuff and things out of closets that shouldn't have been opened in the first place. They ask more questions and eat more cookies than you can count. They are great at losing boots, one glove, snowcaps, sweatshirts, balls, books, lunch money, and instructions. They are devoted to creatures of the earth that growl, slither, wiggle, snarl, curl, and crawl. Grade-schoolers collect pop, rocks, wrappers, premium baseball cards, drop earrings or ski patches, and pencil stubs. They boast a fan club made up of proud parents and grandparents, teachers, big sisters, and the owner of the local store stocked with after-school treats.

Oh yes, grade-schoolers are for loving, too.

The twelve- to twenty-year-olds in a family grow

*NJO NJO NJO NJO NJO NJO NJO NJO NJO NJO*

too much too soon or too little too late. Their cocoons have some problems, but they become some attractive butterflies when puberty is over. Male or female body beauty reaches its peak then. They win us over with their quick wit, fierce loyalties, and the fact that they remembered our birthdays with an extravagant gift.

Already their wisdom is amazing and their appetites alarming. They are a challenge as well as being challengers. They challenge our authority, our decisions, our life-style, our taste in music, movies, clothing, as well as our turn to have the car, the phone, the bathroom, and the computer.

The twelve-to-twenty people in the family are in and out of love, in and out of work, in and out of the bathroom, the house, the refrigerator, and the piggy bank with alacrity. They move in ultra-drive—five hundred megabytes without crashing and burning. Then one day, too soon, they emerge smarter, stronger, and more spiritual than we. But let us remember that we lifted—dragged, wheedled, whipped, fought, threatened, talked, prayed, and loved them to where they are today. We just won't talk about it in front of them because it will ruin the whole thing.

One thing is certain, in the best of families the twelve-to-twenty people are for loving. Try loving them and see.

Yes, families are God's way of blessing the world while shaping a strong, stubborn male into a sensitive patriarch, and a beautiful, bossy female into a beautiful, blessed mother. Oh, thank God families can be forever.

This essay about families is a reminder of the good times we can have living with each other in spite of the daily hassle of real living.

*NJO  NJO  NJO  NJO  NJO  NJO  NJO  NJO  NJO  NJO*

## A Case Study for Miracles

Families are a case study for miracles. In spite of whatever kind of hardship or lack of knowledge about God's ways, good people can make good things happen when they work together under the same roof, tepee, tent, tenement, grass shack, igloo, thatched cottage, or condo. Acceptance of each other is a beginning. Being dependent on each other follows. Loyalty, love, helpfulness, and holiness are the blessings that come next. These are gifts of God given to those who accept his assignment to unselfishly live in families, to bring forth new members of the human race and help them grow up wonderful.

One of the biggest miracles is today's mixed-up families. Making relationships work well today seems harder than burying the dead on the plains and hitching up your wagon and heading west.

There are no perfect families because families are composed of imperfect people. Even when all are doing their best all the time, there are too many factions at work that disturb perfect relating, peace, and ease, with life exactly the way you want it. You are not the only member of the family with a complaint. Try being a dad or a mom. Frankly, this is why it is so stupid—besides being a sin—to fool around with sex. Sex is the business of babies. Never forget that. Babies are the business of families who have the God-ordained right of growing up wonderful. But they are dependent upon others for realizing that privilege. Unmarried people who have sex for self-gratification are running the risk of ruining life for others. That goes against all God says, all society has discovered, and all that you know in your heart of hearts to be true.

You've heard about the campaigns for saving everything from rain forests to whales, from newspapers to energy. How about going on your own crusade for saving the family?

Start with yours by starting with you. Put into practice all the social graces for making life more comfortable for all concerned. Try the gospel of Jesus Christ in a practical setting—the Beatitudes, the Ten Commandments, the sweet sayings of Jesus, and the wise words of prophets are given to us for our benefit. The whole point of life is to learn to love and to be lovable. First we learn to know and love God and try to become like him. Next we learn to love others—all others—as ourselves.

There are problem people and there are people with problems—of all ages. There are people also who know better than to behave as they do, sometimes, but who simply do not care. These matters are subjects for another book. However, since you may be affected by such situations, we remind you that God's ideal for relationships between people is still valid today. It is better—it is God's will, in fact—that people learn to live together happily. Physical or mental harm are to be avoided, and are to be dealt with, if need be, by proper authorities and without delay.

Now, what do you superb youth do about your special family problems? For example, how does a teenage member of a family handle split religions? once-in-a-while parents? step live-ins? mixed marriage? illegitimate offspring? survival among siblings? the single-parent syndrome?

Today's society is geared up for the families with problems like those listed above. Remember that your bishop was called through the inspiration and influence of the Holy Ghost, a gift from God. He has re-

*NJO  NJO  NJO  NJO  NJO  NJO  NJO  NJO  NJO  NJO*

markable God-given insight, then, for the good of his ward family membership. Let him help you. Also, keep praying that you may behave as a child of God should behave. As a child of God, who is perfect.

He has said we are to be as he is!

He has commanded that we love one another.

He has promised us awesome blessings along the way if we try to be righteous and Christlike. He has not promised us a picnic, smiles instead of tears, perfect relationships, or freedom from sickness and hardship. He has promised us that tough times will be for our growth and good. Ultimate joy comes to those who endure in righteousness.

The gospel principles are practical as well as true—universal and eternal and suitable for all situations. Whatever kind of challenge that we have in a family, applying gospel principles can work. Forgiveness, love, patience, unselfishness, humility, fair play, obedience, and recognition that God loves all of his children are some of the virtues people need to develop for living together in normal affection. The pattern has been set for ideal family life. This includes blood relatives, adopted family members, single-parent homes, mixed marriages, his-hers-and-ours households—whatever the detail is of the family structure. This is true, for example, in a situation where an unwed girl gives birth to a baby. If she prayerfully considers the best thing for the baby, she will turn the illegitimate (or *illegal*) child over to proper authorities to be placed in a *legal* family. If a stepfather is abusive, gospel principles suggest that though the offender should not be judged unfairly, the innocent should be protected against the offender.

Yo, Dad! Hi, Mom! Your **not just ordinary** offspring love you better than ever. As they grow in understanding of the life and the possibilities of people and the heavy, heavy burden of parenting, they value you, appreciate you, and want to help make your family dreams come true, They're committed to doing just that!

Right, boys and girls? (Hey, come on! Say *yes*.)

## You'll Want to Remember . . .

Families have their own personalities. The change in family structure, family relationships, and the roles of various members does not change the Lord's will for his children on earth. The best way to live is in love— love for one another as God's children. It may be a new day, but old ideals and commandments (given for our own good!) still apply. Families are meant to be havens of peace and love, with eternal promises at the top of their list.

You want to be part of an eternal family. But no one can force anyone into heaven on earth or after death. People make their own peace by working closely with the Lord, applying his principles to life.

Considering this, is there anything specific that you need to do about yourself, any changes you'd like to make?

*NJO   NJO   NJO   NJO   NJO   NJO   NJO   NJO   NJO   NJO*

# CHAPTER
## 7

# *A Moving Story*

# A Moving Story

Let's talk about you, one more time! It can be a moving story, with hope for a happy ending. Like, what are you thinking now?

Do you believe that you are really a child of God, our Heavenly Father?

Do you have a testimony that Jesus is the Redeemer and that he lives now?

Have you made an accounting with yourself in terms of your heritage, the family into which you were born—your genes, training, environment?

Are things going the way you want them to? Is life like cruising in the fast lane or more like chug-a-lug-lugging along through the chuckholes?

Have you come to grips with not only who you are but *what* you are?

Are you thinking about becoming even better than you already are? (Let's keep *that* secret, but go for it!)

So, out of the ordinary and wonderful as you are, you may have noted that you aren't perfect. Well, of course not. Who is—yet? Perhaps you have become

*NJO   NJO   NJO   NJO   NJO   NJO   NJO   NJO   NJO   NJO*

convinced, at this growing-up stage of your life, that you *want* to change some things yourself in your life.

Maybe you have picked up a bad habit, learned some four-letter words out in the world wherever. Hey, maybe you have aped a negative influence from family and friends. It could be that you are sinning a little or a lot because you do not know how to deal with temptations and problems and peer pressure. Maybe you keep pulling a no-win scenario in the human relationship category. Like at home, for example.

## How Does Change Happen?

Okay, Mom's always talking to you about change: changing your sweats, your hairdo, your bedtime routine and wake-up calls, your grade point, your friends, your manners and your messy projects, your lazy ways and the music you listen to, your monopoly of the telephone, the bathroom, the family car, and everybody's attention.

It may sound far out, but for starters compare yourself to the standard set by Jesus. As wonderful as you are, you probably have a way to go before you will be as he is—as he wants you to be. If you want to become even better than you already are, effort is the next big move to make. We aren't talking perfection here; it's more like personal progress.

This approach is about becoming the kind of growing person who is also a catalyst for change among others.

Here are six supersteps toward changing oneself. If you have studied first aid you know that no Band-Aid treatment can patch up your progress. However, following these six supersteps holds real promise. You

*NJO NJO NJO NJO NJO NJO NJO NJO NJO NJO*

see, the life you save just may be your own. Now, that's spiritual first aid.

1. *Call up your own personal power source*

This is a critical step. For a moment, seek deep within you to a point of conviction about who you really are. Be still and listen! As the Holy Ghost witnesses to your spirit that you *are* a child of God, you will suddenly realize what a difference that makes. Faith in yourself is important. More times than not, self-awareness and self-esteem are the sweepstakes in personal progress and a "happy days are here again" outlook.

And keep your own counsel. That means to listen to yourself. You have been taught correct principles. You know more than you know you know! Your 'spiritual microchip' came to earth with you, and you need to be reassured about why you are **not just** an **ordinary** guy or girl. While you are getting there, hold sacred the details of your life—don't blab to your peers your problem or your plans. Keep cool. Keep it impersonal until the time of sharing is appropriate. In other words, give yourself a chance to grow in a better direction before the whole crowd gets on your case.

2. *Consider the heavenly connection*

The safest way to get something off your chest is through the privacy of prayer. It's called the heavenly connection. You can talk about anything—anything at all—with your Heavenly Father.

Try it and see how good it is!

You are wise to consult your ultimate power source—Heavenly Father. After all, he *is* your Heavenly Father. He gave you life, established this world and its systems for your life. Never forget that. You know that your computer can't do much unless it is plugged in to its power source. And if the power source is interrupted you can lose all that you have been working on. Get the picture?

So you pray daily. On your knees, in formal respect to Heavenly Father—and to keep you awake.

You pray for guidance, you listen for some promptings about direction.

You pray to resist temptation, and your spine turns to steel.

You pray for zest to start over if you make a misstep, and you feel God's assurance that *you* are worth the effort.

Pray earnestly, believing God is there, and you'll feel that he is. It may take a while to recognize what's happening if you are out of practice. But keep at it, as you would if you were sharpening your waterskiing skills.

From here to eternity is a long, long time (unless the alternative gets in the way!), so you pray for patience to hang on while the unfolding of change within you happens.

See that it does, because your life depends on it!

Mark Twain's *Adventures of Huckleberry Finn* casts a light on the matter of prayer when Huck says: "I was letting *on* to give up sin, but away inside of me I was holding on to the biggest one of all. I was trying to make my mouth *say* I would do the right thing and the clean thing, . . . but deep down in me I knowed it was a lie, and He knowed it. You can't pray a lie—I found that out."[14]

3. *Help! Help!*

Parents and others want to help youth. Some of them think it is their sole purpose in life, at least that is the way they talk. And yes, you have your agency— when the talk starts you can go into your room and slam the door or slide on your headphones.

Or you can stick around and listen. You know, make friends with them. You might learn something. Besides, they're trying so hard. For you and your problems they will even set aside their favorite pursuits, such as golf, ironing, genealogy, weeding the garden, folding the laundry, reconciling the checks, and all that fun stuff. All for you!

Did you know that one of these days parents will have to account before God for their part in your earthly life? They must make a report of their stewardship over you, one of Heavenly Father's **not just ordinary** spirit children! You know they are legally responsible for you. Parents—bless 'em—are bent on protecting you against today's porno artists and video voyeurs, crime rate and gang wars, legislation and court systems. Parents love you in a way you will never understand until you have a child of your own.

If you can feel comfortable talking to them (oh, try!), discuss with your parents your desire to change. Or perhaps you'd choose to confide in a teacher, a Church leader, a doctor, a school counselor. A trusted older sibling or friend who has experienced and is concerned for you can be a mighty helpful friend to you now.

Remember—always remember—that one of these days your parents will have to account before God for their part in your earthly life. And again, always remember that your parents love you in a way you'll never understand until you have a child of your own.

4. *Get information to act upon*

Seek *truth* for *your* life.

Find out what's right and what's wrong, what's smart and what's stupid or sinful.

Get ideas through reading the scriptures and other relevant materials from Church literature and library

*NJO NJO NJO NJO NJO NJO NJO NJO NJO NJO*

sources. There is a lot of stuff out there to read, so you better be selective or you'll be so busy reading you'll miss the prom or starve to death.

Here's that word again, that great advice—*pray*. Pray that you may be led to helpful sources, and pray for understanding as you study.

5. *Recycle your thinking*

Yes. Yes, indeed. Recycle your thinking that so far hasn't turned you into the "unisex perfect kid." Get a new perspective.

Get a new perspective for a better you.

Recycle your thinking and resurrect the beautiful expressions, the people-pleasing phrases, the Golden Rule touches. Oh, what a lovely life it is when people remember to say "Please," "Thank you," "I'm sorry," "It's my fault," "No problem," "Let's forget it," "You are great," "Excuse me!"

So get information to act upon. Get serious about getting better. You learn to swim so that you won't drown, right? And you took driver's training before getting the "big license." You sign up for ski lessons to prevent a broken leg. Learn how to live, really live, by getting the right information to act upon.

6. *Live smart*

Live smart, as a **not just ordinary** Young Man or Young Woman should.

Live by your convictions.

Live by your promises and covenants with God.

In seeking for spiritual change and growth, you are considering the six supersteps. As you follow this system or some other great change method, you'll acquire new values, or the old familiar ones will be underscored. This is just the kind of information you need in order to be what you want to be when you want to be it.

*NJO NJO NJO NJO NJO NJO NJO NJO NJO NJO*

Experiment upon the truth as you've pulled it up again. Don't do anything without the test question, "Is this right for *me?*" Trash the rest of the world and its mistaken viewpoints. Ask, "What does Heavenly Father want *me* to do (say, think, feel)?" As you focus your mind and efforts in this way, you become ever closer to the ideal. "What manner of men [boys and girls] ought ye to be? Verily I say unto you, even as I am." (3 Nephi 27:27.) Now, that is a stunner.

Remember, you aren't going to all this trouble for just a youth talk in seminary or something! This is your one chance to live on planet Earth.

## The Other Side of Now

The day you wake up thrilled with the progress you are making is the day you become a servant of the Lord. That day is the other side of now—now that you've grown up wonderful!

- Now you can share what you've learned.
- Already you can be a kind of missionary or special helper.
- You are a good example in word, in conversation, in charity, in spirit, in faith, in purity.
- You've decided to neglect not the gift of the Holy Ghost within you. (Does that sound like familiar scripture? It is; you'll find more about it in the Bible, 1 Timothy 4:14.)
- To your friends you can present the remarkable opportunities for choice, the satisfying alternatives in a young life.
- When the time is right and as the Spirit moves you, you can be a witness of Jesus. You can testify of God's goodness in forgiving and inspiring

*NJO NJO NJO NJO NJO NJO NJO NJO NJO NJO*

and protecting—and comforting and loving! You can testify that he lives! And that makes all the difference.

## You'll Want to Remember . . .

God knows what you are going through. While on the earth Jesus was tempted in *his* areas just as you will be tempted in yours. You can count on it. Jesus resisted and rose above it. So must you. Turn to the Lord for help. He is waiting.

Your loving elders know what you are going through. Parents and leaders have learned about life on "Heartbreak Hill." They've suffered, they've struggled, they've paid a price for being where they are today. Let them help you.

You know something about life and its trials and temptations; about the way fun times can have a dark side; and about how tough it is to do what you know you ought to for your own good, your own joy, your own future. The Holy Ghost will help you know unequivocally right from wrong. Your personal strength can help you do what is right and smart.

You are **not just ordinary** Young Men and Young Women. You keep your goal highlighted: "Become as Jesus is." That requires change. It is a moving story. It is an ongoing pursuit. But with God, nothing is impossible, and so you put your hand in his, so to speak, and you move forward.

The six supersteps to change are:

1. Call up your own personal power source
2  Consider the heavenly connection
3. Help! Help!

*NJO  NJO  NJO  NJO  NJO  NJO  NJO  NJO  NJO  NJO*

4. Get information to act upon
5. Recycle your thinking
6. Live smart

May this moving story have a happy ending for you.

# CHAPTER
## 8

# *The No-Nonsense Life-Style*

# The No-Nonsense Life-Style

You have heard it said that there is good news and bad news.

The bad news is that a lot of people are frustrated and confused. They are printing their life story in the wrong font.

At school you may have studied the history of the "seven deadly sins." Maybe you heard about them from friends in another religious group. Could be your seminary teacher referred to them.

For your information, the seven deadly sins are pride, covetousness, lust, anger, gluttony, envy, and sloth. Since the sixth century, representations of these blights on man's character have been featured in art and literature. But over the generations such representations haven't seemed to help anybody much.

You know the stories of the generations—wars and rumors of war, pride going before the fall, anger breaking up homes, lust getting missionaries dishonorably released—that kind of needless harmful happening.

The pits, mankind. Off to the pits! Forty days of rain!

Life is a trial.

That's the bad news.

Now, for the good news.

The good news is that life *can* be lived with fewer heartaches. We are talking *help*.

The good news is that there are answers to life's situations, whatever they might be at your stage of the game. You name it. For starters, how about these situations: being diagnosed with leukemia in your junior year; your dad has married again and the lady is a Cinderella's-stepmother type without even trying to be; you have turned sixteen and your mom won't let you get your driver's license for two more years; your friend is into drinking, drugs, shoplifting, sex, and is hassling *you* (this is a friend?).

Wait! Wait! There is good news to help you. There is a mighty support system for those like you who are seeking the no-nonsense life-style. Which, of course, doesn't forestall tests, tears, heartbreak, suffering, disappointment, and your favorite friend doing the prom with somebody else. But it surely helps.

The good news is that there is a selection of information that can save mankind.

Go shout it from the mountain!

Go teach it in the town square!

Go hang it from the billboards.

At least, guys and girls, base some of your youth talks around that most important discovery in all time toward achieving a no-nonsense life-style and no unnecessary frustration and pain—the vital system for living given by God to Joseph Smith when he was *your* age. He was given the facts that help people cope with this life happily and make it to the next one with confidence.

*NJO  NJO  NJO  NJO  NJO  NJO  NJO  NJO  NJO  NJO*

The good news is that the gospel of God is a blessing among us.

*Gospel* means "good news."

The good news is that the gospel is the word of God. God is your creator. He knows what you need. You need the gospel for a great life. Got it?

Now, where do you find the word of God to help you live the no-nonsense life-style?

From parents? Hopefully. If yours didn't know about things like this, prepare yourself to know things like this for your own children.

From schoolteachers? Well, it would be great if you always could. But can you be sure you are getting truth from someone who knows only part of the story of God, man, and the plan?

From institutions? Maybe. Provided you come under the influence of the right institution. Public schools are tangled in legalities. The supposed rights of others may limit your growth. You, after all, are **not just ordinary** Young Men and Young Women. You need more information about the purpose of life and the plan to follow for success and some peace.

You need the whole truth and nothing but the truth for that all-important no-nonsense life-style.

A no-nonsense life-style is living by standards that keep you comfortable before God and out of trouble. This isn't about not having any fun; you don't have to be cut off from excitement or growth, limited to a nun's or monk's life. No way.

You are looking for joy, not instant gratification. You are dreaming of making a difference in the world —or a corner of it—not messing around all weekend.

You have a particular way of life to live (lucky one); a mission to perform; responsibility to take; more covenants to make with God; the temple endowment to prepare for; a forever marriage to look forward to,

*NJO   NJO   NJO   NJO   NJO   NJO   NJO   NJO   NJO   NJO*

performed by one having authority. And the next generation to rear in righteousness.

Ready or not, your day is upon you. Remember if you can. Cram if you must. But get on with the no-nonsense, no-detours, no-stupid-stuff march down life's path.

The good word for you is to abide in the liberty that ensures freedom of choice by not entangling yourself in sin. To do this you need all of the word of God—all the good news—available on earth at this time.

The word of God comes in a colorful, convenient variety of forms. Find the source you can easily turn to, understand, never forget, and valiantly live by.

Consider these sources for acquiring the knowledge you need—the information that you are entitled to, given who you are as **not just ordinary** Young Men and Young Women:

- Sacrament meeting
- Priesthood quorum
- Young women meetings
- Seminary and institute classes
- The scriptures—Old and New Testaments, the Book of Mormon, the Doctrine and Covenants, the Pearl of Great Price
- Support material found in excellent Church books by LDS authors, available through Church distribution centers, or your local LDS bookstore (usually near a temple) or book club
- Church magazines
- Manuals and materials prepared for the various departments and age-groups of the Church
- The *Church News*, published weekly in the *Deseret News*
- Conference reports in published form, on video, or on audiotapes

*NJO  NJO  NJO  NJO  NJO  NJO  NJO  NJO  NJO  NJO*

- Lectures sponsored by the Church Educational System
- Church-sponsored firesides, youth conferences, devotionals
- Personal conversation with stalwart leaders, friends, family
- Prayer; through the power of the Holy Ghost your spirit may be taught wonderful things— ask and you shall receive
- *For the Strength of Youth,* the current pamphlet for the Church program to boost and bolster **not just ordinary** Young Men and Young Women

## You'll Want to Remember . . .

The no-nonsense life-style is about standards, correct principles, doing more things right and fewer things wrong.

You **not just ordinary** Young Men and Young Women seem to have correct principles deeply rooted in you—the *you* being your soul, your mind and brain. To have deeply rooted standards in this sense is to feel passionately about principles that enable you to govern yourself wisely.

If you know good from bad, best from better, right from wrong, strength from sin, and if you *perform* accordingly, you will avoid unnecessary trouble, frustration, and disciplinary action by Church or state.

You can be of good use to your friends, as well. You can't nag anyone into smart stuff, but you can stand by, offer alternatives, present the good news that the no-nonsense life-style is the only way to go.

There is good news to help you work your way

*NJO   NJO   NJO   NJO   NJO   NJO   NJO   NJO   NJO   NJO*

through life. There are ways to improve your moments and make them shining. There are principles, people, and publications to keep you on track.

And for all you **not just ordinary** Young Men and Young Women there are some absolutes to live by.

*NJO  NJO  NJO  NJO  NJO  NJO  NJO  NJO  NJO  NJO*

# CHAPTER
## 9

# *The Absolutes*

# The Absolutes

Absolutes? For your particular life? Absolutely!

There are a lot of rules in life. There are some good ideas, important commandments, and there are some absolutes that can be beneficial to your personal progress. You have to pay attention to them, however, because they won't work within you automatically or by osmosis.

Here we go!

*Never underestimate the value of the absolutes!*

*You are never a loser until you quit trying; you are never a winner unless you start.*

*Never underestimate the power of God.*

*Never forget that Satan wants you.*

*Just being alive is awesome. It's the ultimate adventure. Don't blow it!*

*NJO   NJO   NJO   NJO   NJO   NJO   NJO   NJO   NJO   NJO*

*Hell is definitely not where you want to go. Procrastinating the day of repenting is risky business. You never know when you will die.*

*You are only young once, and this is the growing time—grow up good, or grow up malformed because of your response to life's enticements. Put up the dukes, youth! Satan is at war with you. Since you want and need to be a spiritual athlete, you'll have to train for it.*

*Life comes one to a customer. Only you can ruin it.*

*There are two great hypocrisies: thinking you are more than you are (that you are somehow immune to sin), and thinking you are less than you are (that you are anything other than a child of God).*

*Never forget that Satan is real, and that he is working overtime-and-a-half in this world to spread foolishness as well as evil.*

*There will be wonderful surprises all along the way when you truly believe in God.*

*NJO   NJO   NJO   NJO   NJO   NJO   NJO   NJO   NJO   NJO*

*Heeding the guidelines for gaining real personal strength brings personal strength as well as peace of mind.*

*Heavenly Father has never told you to do something that wasn't good for you or not to do something that was.*

*Three things to understand: covenants, how to cultivate the Holy Ghost, and the importance of taking control of your own life.*

*When you live the precious legend, you can count on remarkable results.*

*Because of who you are, the mission of your life span on earth, the promises you have made, and the power you have been given—because of these things life will be different for you. So will the hereafter.*

*Never forget that you are* **not just ordinary** *Young Men and Young Women.*

*Hold on to dear life— fasten your seat belt, put on your life jacket, your riding helmet, your running shoes. And keep your hand in the Lord's, too.*

*NJO NJO NJO NJO NJO NJO NJO NJO NJO NJO*

*Sin is not a bowl of cherries. It is more like wallowing in the pits.*

*The key to self-mastery comes by studying your own life, your own desires and wants, cravings and temptations to bring them under control.*

*Suicide is stupid. Absolutely deadly. It is no way out of trouble for anybody—let alone you **not just ordinary** Young Men and Young Women.*

*He that hath clean hands and a pure heart is loved by the Lord (see Psalm 24:3–4). He that hath clean hands, knuckles, and fingernails is loved by the congregation to whom he passes the sacrament.*

*Listen to the prophet's voice. He has something to say to you.*

*If you are cleansed from all sin, you can ask of God whatsoever you will and in the name of Jesus Christ it shall be done.*

*If you draw near to God, your loving and all-knowing Heavenly Father, he will surely draw near to you.*

**NJO** **NJO** **NJO** **NJO** **NJO** **NJO** **NJO** **NJO** **NJO** **NJO**

*If you press toward "the mark," you will meet with unexpected success at unexpected times.*

*Cease to be idle or unclean or to find fault with one another; arise early and retire on time, ceasing to sleep longer than is necessary, and this that your minds and bodies may be invigorated (see D&C 88:124).*

*Something to do, someone to love, and something to hope for make life worthwhile.*

*When you want to stay in control and out of trouble—worthy, confident before God, and in touch with your parents—learn to say no to the stupid stuff and yes to the growing opportunities.*

*Christ's kind of "Christianity" (or religion) contains the answers to the moral problems of mankind. You have a critical and vital opportunity to be a kind of missionary to spread this good news.*

*Abstinence makes the heart grow stronger.*

NJO NJO NJO NJO NJO NJO NJO NJO NJO NJO

*Instant gratification (sex, spending money, goofing off at school) may seem promising at first—but in the long run it can bring personal ruin.*

*Don't miss what matters! It's your choice. Whatever happens outside in the world, inside yourself you have control.*

*Chastity is a better program than abortion.*

*Suddenly you learn that if you want to be treated like an adult you have to act as if you are one.*

*Clean up your act, and while you are at it clean up your room. The Spirit of the Lord can't dwell in an unclean being or bedroom.*

*No no-no's keeps your sleep sweet.*

*People who know where they are going and what they are doing usually get there.*

*NJO   NJO   NJO   NJO   NJO   NJO   NJO   NJO   NJO   NJC*

*Smoking should not be a part of growing up. Smoking, drinking beer and liquor, doing drugs, being unchaste, heeding mind-frying messages shouldn't be part of any time in your life.*

*Life is school. There will be tests and trials. There will be dunner days. With God you can have stunner days.*

*You are what you eat, read, think, hear, see, and do.*

*Don't play as if you're married when you are not and as if you're not when you are.*

*Be strong and of good courage; be not afraid, and don't feel dismayed: for the Lord is with you wherever you go, if you want.*

*A true friend shows up when everyone else has bowed out. Find one. Be one.*

*All the right moves bring all the right results. It's the law of the harvest: If you plant parsley seeds, don't expect to reap daisies.*

*You can't fool with evil and feel good.*

*If you want to have friends, be one!*

*A life recorded is a life twice lived.*

*Do what God says and there will be fabulous surprises!*

*It's His world. You are His. But it's your choice for your life.*

*People (and God) appreciate people who have an attitude of gratitude. It is more fun to give, help, comfort, and guide those who receive with thanks.*

*What can you do for someone who saved your life? Always remember him!*

*You can either react or act to what happens to you. Having information to act upon insures appropriate protection to eternal growth.*

*God the Father is your Heavenly Father, too.*

NJO   NJO   NJO   NJO   NJO   NJO   NJO   NJO   NJO   NJO

*You are a spirit child of God the Father. There is a spark of the divine in you. Each person has a physical body to house his or her eternal, unique spirit.*

*He wants you to obey. He wants you to make it—make it in this life and make it back to His presence—and have a super-special, sin-free time doing it!*

*Jesus Christ lives and operates in our lives. He is our spirit brother, the firstborn of our Heavenly Father's spirit children. He is our Redeemer and Savior, our example, teacher, and helper, our friend. He is at the head of his church on earth, which is where we can learn what we need to do in order to go "home" to heaven one day.*

*Earth life comes only once per person to live, learn, do, and then die. It isn't if you die, it's when. Ready, get set . . . go!*

*Your own dearest desires, your highest hopes—your own field of dreams—can be realized.*

NJO NJO NJO NJO NJO NJO NJO NJO NJO NJO

# CHAPTER
## 10

# *Your Own Field of Dreams*

# *Your Own Field of Dreams*

"Mom!" called Peter. "Mom, I want to show you something. Look at this!" Peter put the Bible close to his mother's ironing board as she prepared the family clothing for church the next day.

"What are you so excited about?" She laughed and teased him a bit about reading the scriptures instead of mowing the lawn. "One of these days, Hercules, you'll be reading the scriptures instead of working out. Whatever will become of us?"

"Mom, you are cool. I mean, really cool." And he brushed her cheek with a kiss.

"Hmm. Nice! Well, you must be excited. I haven't had that kind of a treat in a long time."

"Ah, I just don't want to spoil you, that's all. Listen, Mom, you know that new job I have? Well, I figured that if I handled things real carefully, I just might be able to save enough to get into college this fall."

"Are you sure? I wish your father and I could help."

"Oh, that's okay. Don't you worry about that. But I really want to go, you know, and I figured that I'd put every possible cent of my paycheck into savings. I had even decided that I wouldn't pay tithing. I mean, my reason is a good one—saving for college and all. I thought for sure the Lord would understand."

"The Lord might understand, but your dad and I never would. A principle is a principle, Peter, no matter how good an excuse you think you might have for abandoning it."

"I know, I know. Just simmer down. I've been struggling with this for a couple of days. That's why I was studying the scriptures this morning. And look at what I found!" Peter pointed his finger to Malachi 3:10, and together they read out loud:

"Bring ye all the tithes into the storehouse, that there may be meat in mine house, and prove me now herewith, saith the Lord of hosts, if I will not open you the windows of heaven, and pour you out a blessing, that there shall not be room enough to receive it."

"That's impressive, isn't it?" asked Peter's mother, relieved.

"Impressive? It's like WOW!" exclaimed Peter. "Honest, Mom, when I read that scripture it blazed up in my mind like fireworks."

"So what are you going to do about it?"

"That's just it. I think I've changed my mind. I think I'll pay my tithing and claim my blessings."

"Hold on, there, Peter. Before you have your heart set and get disappointed, let me tell you something that I've learned in life that seems relevant here. The Lord does hear and answer our prayers. He does pour us out a blessing, sooner or later, but it may not be exactly the kind of blessing we had in mind."

"Oh, Mom!" Peter sighed, thinking that adults could sometimes be a real drag.

"Wait!" Peter's mother insisted. "If we say 'thy will be done' and we understand that the Lord knows what

*NJO  NJO  NJO  NJO  NJO  NJO  NJO  NJO  NJO  NJC*

is best for us, it will be all right, whatever happens. Sometimes we have to learn later why our prayer was answered the way it was."

"Hmm. Yeah." Peter wilted, and muffled his words with his chin on his chest.

"Peter? Peter, listen to me," said his mother. She set her iron up on end and moved over to place a hand on Peter's shoulder. "Peter, I didn't mean to squelch your joy. This thing is between you and the Lord. I just wanted to give you some perspective I've gained in facing the realities in life."

Inwardly Peter's mother marveled at the inevitable, incredible, invincible faith of youth. *How much we can learn from them!* she thought.

Peter remained quiet a moment, and then he spoke slowly, firmly. His early exuberance was replaced by a certain sober conviction. "Mother, thanks for what you've said about how you feel."

"I love you, Peter," she interrupted.

"Sure, I know that. But it's just that I am sure this scripture was meant for me. Now! I am going to accept the challenge and take the Lord at his word and *prove* him."

"You'll pay your tithing?"

"Yes, Mom, I'll pay my tithing and I expect to be blessed. I think I will have the tuition for college this fall."

And he did.

## When Particular Help Is Needed

We all have remarkable blessings in our lives. Some summer night gather your friends around the bonfire and play the game of counting blessings. You'll learn great stuff about these people with whom you play soccer, fill priesthood assignments, dance, or plan youth meetings. As stated before in these pages, there is no more privileged group of teenagers in the world than you who are **not just ordinary** Young Men and Young Women, and this by virtue of your Church membership and your special covenants and what you know about the meaning of life. So count your many blessings and be thankful.

Often, though, particular help is needed. A young friend of mine reported on a choice experience he had with one of the General Authorities of the Church. Jim wanted to get a new perspective on a problem. He explained his need, and the General Authority responded, "I know what you are feeling, Jim. I look back on my life's experiences and can't begin to count all the prayers I've offered for help. And I've received helpful answers. Along the way I have learned a thing or two that might be helpful to you."

"I'd be grateful for anything you can tell me. The more I think about my problem, the more confused I seem to get. I keep thinking that Heavenly Father and Jesus must be sick of me," confessed Jim.

"Nah. They aren't sick of you. They love you. The Lord wants us to struggle and grow and learn from our trials and problems. So we pray for guidance and strength, and then we try to work our way through the immediate challenges. God doesn't function like a quick-change artist. Okay?"

"Okay."

"Now and then I have faced a problem and I have checked my personal resources (my talents and so on) for solving it. If I am lacking in some particular way to bring about a desired outcome, I go humbly before the Lord, admitting my weakness and explaining my need. I actually ask for a gift from God."

*NJO NJO NJO NJO NJO NJO NJO NJO NJO NJO*

"You do, really? That seems daring to me." Jim was fascinated by all this and appreciated the candor of this great young leader in the high ranks of the Church.

"It *is* daring. But I have come to know God. I know I can count on him to help me if I do all that I can. Jim, do you recall that young King Solomon asked God for an 'understanding heart' so that he could rule the people wisely?"

"Sure, I remember that story."

"Isn't that a plea for a special gift to fit a certain circumstance?"

"Yes."

"Well, in a certain situation I, too, have earnestly prayed for a gift. I've said something like, 'O dear Heavenly Father, my own resources aren't enough. I need a gift from thee. A gift!' "

"That's startling to me. What is an example of this?"

"For example, the gift of discernment, so that I could perceive the details of a problem beyond what I might normally be able to do."

"That's great. But you and King Solomon are out of my league. You are a special servant of the Lord. Of course *your* prayers would be answered," observed Jim.

"So will yours, Jim. You, too, are a special servant of the Lord. In his kingdom on earth you also have a certain work to do—you are not just an ordinary young man who doesn't understand what life is all about!"

"Awesome! You put a new slant on praying."

"I'm a father of several children. Family life presents plenty of opportunities to turn to heaven for blessings! You know, Jim, I love my children. I want to help them. I'd do anything for them, but I don't want to spoil them, or deprive them of growth that comes from their working things through for themselves. I know that I shouldn't deny them their agency, either. But if they are doing the right things, if they humbly admit their need, and if they have a grateful spirit about my place in their lives—I want to help them. I recognize their readiness to be given special treatment."

"What you are telling me is that earthly and Heavenly fathers aren't all that different when it comes to helping their children?"

"Only in degree, I'd say, and spiritual insight. God, after all, can see the end from the beginning."

"Thank you for this conversation. I'll work on my humility and—"

"Humility, Jim, follows naturally after gratitude!" added the older man.

"Got it!"

## Blessings You Don't Have to Ask for

Some blessings you don't even have to ask for— God is *that* good! They come by virtue of your being involved in the Church of Jesus Christ today. It begins with being born and ends with the dedication of the grave you are buried in.

Blessing? What exactly is a *blessing?* It is a sacred favor from Deity, anything that brings joy or goodness into life. It is a way of setting a person apart from the world and bestowing well-being, opportunity, and enlightenment. It makes life flow more smoothly. A blessing brings peace.

You are **not just ordinary** Young Men and Young Women, because from the beginning you were prayed over and given a name and a blessing. Likely as not, your mother was given a priesthood blessing before she went into labor at your birth. If that wasn't the case, keep it in mind for your own life and your own children. It is a very tender closeness that develops on such an important occasion when a young husband places his hands upon his wife's head and gives her a blessing to strengthen and protect her in the hours of giving birth.

Ideally a baby is brought before the Church soon after it is born, to be given a name and a blessing. The proper Church records are then made to preserve genealogical information. The blessing itself, while it is not an ordinance of salvation per se, gives the child a great spiritual start in life and is a comforting guide to the parents and family of the newborn. While the child is not subject to the devil's influence until the age of eight, promises of protection against evil and ill health are often included in this blessing. Someone holding the Melchizedek Priesthood is voice for the blessing and, in most cases, it is the father himself.

## Christ Blessed the Little Children

During the time of Christ's mortal ministry, people brought their little children to him that he might lay his hands upon them. The disciples rebuked the people saying, "There is no need, for Jesus hath said, Such shall be saved." But Jesus himself then answered and said, "Suffer little children to come unto me, and forbid them not, for of such is the kingdom of heaven. And he laid hands on them." (JST, Matthew 19:13–15.)

When Christ was teaching among the people on the ancient American continent, he directed the people to ponder his words and to pray for understanding. Then he, himself, prayed unto Heavenly Father for all these good people. The angels of heaven came down and ministered to their little ones, and the children were encircled with fire, as well. Fire is a symbol of the power of the Holy Ghost, and the people made record of this marvelous miracle that was a blessing in all of their lives.

At any needful time in your life—as often as necessary in times of sickness or affliction—you may receive the ordinance of administration for the healing of the sick. Through the laying on of hands by priesthood bearers you can be anointed with consecrated oil by one man; that anointing is then sealed, and a blessing added, by one or more men.

When a baptized person is confirmed a member of The Church of Jesus Christ of Latter-day Saints, the Holy Ghost is given or bestowed. This is done by the laying on of hands by priesthood bearers and is usually followed by a blessing with promises and guidance for the benefit of that individual.

Boys receive the choice blessing of the Aaronic Priesthood at age twelve, and at about nineteen years of age they receive the Melchizedek Priesthood. These priesthood conferrals are given by the laying on of hands and through the power of the priesthood of God. Sometimes girls over twelve who are involved in the Young Women program of the Church are given blessings when they are set apart as class officers.

A patriarchal blessing is yours to have when you are ready for it. Based upon your worthiness as determined through a personal interview, the bishop will give you a recommend to take to the stake patriarch at the time of your blessing. This is a unique privilege reserved for you **not so ordinary** Young Men and Young Women who are members of The Church of Jesus Christ of Latter-day Saints. It is one more thing that

*NJO  NJO  NJO  NJO  NJO  NJO  NJO  NJO  NJO  NJC*

the Lord Jesus has in store for us. Part of your preparing for this experience is to fast and pray, to repent before God, and to ask for understanding for yourself and inspiration for the patriarch. How wonderful to learn what Heavenly Father has in store for you personally! This is not the patriarch's blessing for you, it is God's! Never forget that. Once you have your blessing, keep it safe and secret. Read and live by it. Use it as a guide for decision making and for avoiding pitfalls or detours in your life, as well as for goal setting and joyful anticipation.

A father's blessing is a very special happening in the household of faith. This is when your own father— or grandfather, perhaps—lays his hands upon your head and unfolds hope, helpful promises, and love at a special time in your life. It can happen when you are going off to school or a mission, starting a new job, leaving home, getting married, trying to repent and start a new life.

There are other specific blessings in store for you that come with maturity. Elder Bruce R. McConkie wrote the following helpful information for you to think about: "Among his laws and commandments, the Lord has provided certain rites and ceremonies which are also called ordinances. These ordinance-rites might be pictured as a small circle within the larger circle of ordinance-commandments. Most of these rites and ceremonies, as illustrated by baptism and celestial marriage, are essential to salvation and exaltation in the kingdom of God; some of them, such as the blessing of children and the dedication of graves, are not ordinances of salvation, but are performed for the comfort, consolation, and encouragement of the saints."[15]

"I will . . . open you the windows of heaven, and pour you out a blessing, that there shall not be room enough to receive it" (Malachi 3:10). You can count on

*NJO NJO NJO NJO NJO NJO NJO NJO NJO NJO*

the Lord; he has forgotten nothing to make life marvelous for us, to boost us through the experience of living in a real world with temptations and troubles to
kick us along the way. But the Lord is there for us.
Guidance, comfort, healing, protection, miracles and
messages of truth, saving ordinances that set us apart
with special insights and understandings—all this and
more for strength and well-being.

What a field of rare dreams life is, then!

Now, what about thanksgiving and praise for such
an awesome blessing in our lives as knowing that we
are beloved children of God himself? What about his
special word that seems particularly pointed to you?

# CHAPTER
## 11

# *You Can Believe This!*

# You Can Believe This!

When you feel yourself being roped into something you aren't sure about, likely you will agree that life is a tug-of-war of sorts. When the powers of God are pulling one way and the forces of evil are yanking another, it can be frightening and frustrating.

No childhood game, this! Serious adult decisions are under way and you need help—rules to live by, crutches, support systems, cheering sections, or whatever—to keep you out of trouble and into happiness.

All right—you can believe this!

The following terrific truths are especially for you. They are perfect help for this time in your life.

Call them guidelines.

Call them smart advice.

Call them practical approaches to your grown-up life.

Call them help when you feel helpless.

Call them strength for your weak moments.

Call them commandments or God's laws. Just don't forget to live by them. You can believe this—these good thoughts were written especially for you.

Remember, you are **not just ordinary** Young Men and Young Women. You need particularly pointed counsel to help you reach your full potential, to insure that you'll realize the purpose for being on earth. You have a mission to perform, and these brilliant excerpts from the holy scriptures are just what the Creator, Jesus Christ, had in mind to help you do and help you be what you are supposed to do and be.

You need to be on the Lord's wavelength, following his direction. If you are lazy about getting his word, you just might listen to Satan's subtle taunts. Some people get so sucked under that they don't even recognize the baloney-lies as coming from the other side of darkness.

If you aren't in God's arena you'll be in Satan's. That's an absolute. That's not only a fact, it's a scary fact! You know, that's when you are in for disappointment or heartbreak.

Why, you could take a misstep, commit a stupid sin, make a life-wrecking move, confuse wickedness with happiness!

Plus, you could miss the whole wonderful show of your one chance to live, all because you didn't know enough to make smart choices. All because you didn't know and/or didn't follow "Thy will be done!" Oh, yes, "Thy will be done"—a nice way to close a prayer, but if you don't understand what God's will is and what makes his world work and why he has established certain safeguards and issued certain commandments . . .

Consider these truths. Look them up in your own scriptures. Underline them. Put them to work in your daily life. Pray about them so that you'll get the meaning behind the words, too. This is called reading the white space or reading between the lines.

NJO  NJO  NJO  NJO  NJO  NJO  NJO  NJO  NJO  NJO

Let's go for it! Let's get ready for the rewards (blessings from God!) of living a great earth life according to the rules explained by the Creator himself. After all, you take skiing lessons from a pro, you learn math and grammar at school, you take computer science in college, all so that you can apply that how-to knowledge in your life's activities. But your eternal spirit needs some special learning, too. You have Satan working on you, trying to lure you away from the path that leads back to Heavenly Father's presence—yeah, Satan as well as "friends" and conniving media people who just don't know any better. Well, *you* had better know better.

The word of God, the scriptures themselves, are the operator's manual of instruction for successful operation in life! Scriptures and the current teachings revealed from God through his prophets on earth today are it.

Consider these scriptures especially selected for your generation of **not just ordinary** Young Men and Young Women.

## The Value in Obedience

1 Nephi 3:7. *I will go and do the things which the Lord hath commanded, for I know that the Lord giveth no commandments unto the children of men, save he shall prepare a way for them that they may accomplish the thing which he commandeth them.*

This is wonderful, strengthening scripture. If you memorize it you'll find yourself turning to it mentally again and again when you are tried or tempted. The only things God tells you to abstain from or *not* to do are those things that are damaging, hurtful for your body and spirit. And the things that he commands you *to do* are for your wonderful blessing.

Also, surely someday you'll come up against a situation that seems absolutely rough. Like having to forgive someone who lied about you, or cheated you, or treated you unfairly. Maybe even stole the one you love right away from you. Or like having to "love" your companion, a total stranger (and a bit weird at that, maybe) until you became roomies at the Mission Training Center or the college dorm. Maybe you'll have to set aside a scholarship that you had your heart set on in order to fill a mission with your family or on your own. Maybe you are absolutely the only one among your peers who isn't fooling with drink, drugs, or sex. You want friends, of course, but you don't need to jump off a crazy cliff to destruction just because they try dumb stuff.

You know that 1 Nephi 3:7 has truth for you. The wonder of understanding and believing and living by this scripture is that it works. It works! It promises that God's blessings will pour out upon you and strengthen you.

## Where Strength and Courage Come From

Joshua 1:9. *Be strong and of a good courage; be not afraid, neither be thou dismayed: for the Lord thy God is with thee whithersoever thou goest.*

That is what the Lord said to the prophet Joshua when he was about to lead the children of Israel into

*NJO NJO NJO NJO NJO NJO NJO NJO NJO NJC*

battle. Now, what was good enough for Joshua is good enough for you as you move into the battles of life— you know the kind of battles we're talking about: the filthy words you hear at school; the disgusting disregard some movie and TV directors seem to have for the sacred things of God; the preoccupation with sexual sin of all kinds; the teasing you have to put up with from friends or sometimes even family members who do not understand how deeply you feel about the covenants you've made with Heavenly Father, how much you want to keep them. Well, you can do and be what you want to do and be—with God's help! He has promised you that *wherever* you go he will be with you. You don't have to be afraid, or feel alone, or become confused or even depressed. You go forth with courage and comfort. And hey, it will be okay!

## You—Being About Your Heavenly Father's Business

Joshua 3:5. *Sanctify yourselves: for tomorrow the Lord will do wonders among you.*

Now, there is a stunner.

Imagine, if you get yourself ready, the Lord will work wonders among you and you can work wonders among your friends—with his help, of course.

Ready? How? "Sanctify yourselves," the Lord said. What does *sanctify* mean, exactly?

The dictionary says that *sanctify* has the same Latin root as *saint*. To sanctify is to set apart to a sacred purpose or to religious use; to consecrate; to free from sin; to purify; to make inviolable—which means to make secure against any kind of impurity.

The process of sanctification begins with the ordinances of baptism and confirmation and having the Holy Ghost bestowed upon you. Now you've grown and learned and felt deep and wonderful secrets inside yourself. You've moved forward to receive the priesthood, if you are a boy, or to receive understanding and training about your role as a woman, if you are a girl. You may even have received a patriarchal blessing, which opens up wonderful promises for your life if you keep worthy.

Well, *keep* worthy! Become even more worthy, sanctifying yourselves that you may have the Lord work wonders in your life. There is nothing the world can offer—nothing—that is as important or as satisfying in your life as being part of God's "wonders."

## Is Anybody Perfect?

3 Nephi 12:48. *Therefore I would that ye should be perfect even as I, or your Father who is in heaven is perfect.*

Your goal is to become perfect. *Really* perfect. Jesus taught this. So, you choice and **not just ordinary** Young Men and Young Women, keep growing toward perfection.

Learn his word. Try to live by it.

Study his ways. Try to behave as he did while on earth. You can't imitate Jesus if you don't *know* what he is like. Of course, to *act* like Jesus is only a step toward *being* like Jesus. Way to go, kids.

Pray for his help so you can be strengthened by his power, as he has promised. Remember, you don't have

NJO NJO NJO NJO NJO NJO NJO NJO NJO NJO

to be on your knees to pray for his help, but it's a precious sign of respect and humility to kneel.

You are young, and there is the world full of fascinations. Some "nice" people seem to be involved in things that go against Christ's teaching and the standards of his church on earth. But for someone like you who is trying to become sanctified, even perfect, seeking after the world's delights simply isn't good enough.

Why are you striving for sanctification (granted, this is not something you go shouting about) while you are young? Because tomorrow—if you are ready—the Lord will work wonders through you.

"Oh, come on," you ask, "is anybody perfect?"

Jesus is, and he was while he was on earth. He made the right choices. He resisted terrible temptation. He did much good. He prayed earnestly to Heavenly Father for guidance and strength.

Your blessed opportunity is to become as he is.

## How to Be Like Christ

Doctrine and Covenants 121:45. *Let virtue garnish thy thoughts unceasingly; then shall thy confidence wax strong in the presence of God.*

What we have here is support for the truth that you behave as you think. Now, let's talk about "virtue." What exactly does *virtue* mean? To be virtuous is to be innocent, pure, harmless, good, chaste, without sin, godly. Okay.

Let's talk about "unceasingly." The dictionaries define *unceasingly* as "never stopping, without end." So far we have it that your thoughts are to be pure, guileless, without sin, godly, and that they are never to be anything else. That is, if you are working toward perfection.

Some youths figure they will "fool around" until it is time to go on a mission or go to the temple. That's tough to understand. If you tied a branch to the tree's trunk, or taped one petal to the stem, you end up with a malformed piece of nature. It works that way with any growing thing. Including you. Put a crimp in your own growth for a time and you'll be malformed or scarred. Think about it.

Watch and pray always, that you don't short-circuit your power or mar your spirit. And as you think good thoughts, you can go before Heavenly Father in prayer with confidence, without embarrassment, and the Holy Ghost can be your constant companion.

All *right!*

## Good Versus Not So Good

Alma 41:10. *Behold, I say unto you, wickedness never was happiness.*

Ask anyone who has ever sinned a little or a lot and that person will admit that wickedness never was happiness in the long run. We are children of God; we can't break promises, do foolish or wicked things, and come up smiling. No way! It just doesn't work. There is a way that you can know for sure what is right or wrong, good or terrible. And that's important, because sometimes Satan does clever things, distorting truth so he can get you to trip up and become miserable when all the time you thought you were just in it for a bit of happy fun!

*NJO NJO NJO NJO NJO NJO NJO NJO NJO NJO*

## Nix on Sexual Mischief

**3 Nephi 12:27–28.** *Behold, it is written by them of old time, that thou shalt not commit adultery; but I say unto you, that whosoever looketh on a woman, to lust after her, hath committed adultery already in his heart.*

Nix on adultery—and that goes for any kind of sexual sin. You are not to have sexual relations with anyone to whom you are not properly and legally married. Under the Lord's commandments it has ever been so, and it ever will be!

There's more—if you even *think* evil thoughts, it can be the pits for you!

See no evil, speak no evil, do no evil! Sex is for procreation and procreation is for bringing babies into the world. Yeah, yeah, we know the powerful feelings you have. The sex drive is second only to the drive for survival. Sex has been around forever. You didn't invent it, you know, so why shouldn't you learn from God—whose business procreation is—and others who've already been there?

Oh, wrong ideas may pop into your head. Especially if you watch the wrong kind of movies, listen to the wild music of today, or follow the lead of friends who don't understand the gospel or know Jesus as you do. Quickly put damaging or dirty thoughts out of your mind. Some say it helps to hum a favorite hymn, repeat the memorized scripture, get a mental picture of the temple you want to enter someday. Certainly it helps to silently seek the solace of the Savior in prayer. Remember, you don't have to be on your knees to pray.

# How to Know Right from Wrong

Moroni 7:12, 19. *All things which are good cometh of God; and that which is evil cometh of the devil. . . . Search diligently in the light of Christ that ye may know good from evil.*

That scripture is what I call the "yardstick of judgment." It is a technique for knowing what is right for you to do. Remember, we are talking about *you*. What's okay for ordinary people may not be a good thing for you to be doing, considering you are **not just ordinary** Young Men and Young Women.

For example, if you are invited to go someplace, try something, or be with someone that you aren't sure about, you use that "yardstick of judgment." You see how it measures up to the standard suggested in this wonderful quote from Mormon. Would doing this thing make you feel close to Christ, or is there some doubt? When in doubt, *don't!* It would be a wise move on your part to read all of Moroni 7 very carefully.

Sometimes people make mistakes.

Sometimes people forget who they really are.

Sometimes it is very clear they haven't learned enough, yet, about what works in life and what reaps destruction. What happens if someone gives in to temptation?

# Satan and Sifting

Alma 37:15. *If ye transgress the commandments of God, behold, these things which are sacred shall be taken away from you by the power of God, and ye shall be delivered up unto Satan, that he may sift you as chaff before the wind.*

NJO  NJO  NJO  NJO  NJO  NJO  NJO  NJO  NJO  NJO

Wow! Tough but true.

The answer is there: God is in charge of this world, and he knows what works for the successful life. He has given us his own instruction to help us. Whether others realize these things or not, God is God! He has his own mission to perform, which is to bring about the immortality and eternal life of every person. If we transgress or ignore or sin against his commandments, we are in for real trouble. We'll get *sifted*, so to speak. Good description. Put some wheat kernels in the palm of your hand and grind them about a bit, then slightly open your fingers and let fragments slip through. Open your palm and let the breeze pick up the lightweights—the chaff. Useless stuff.

Sifting. Lightweights are gone! Only useful, heavyweight kernels remain.

Better pray for help, for strength to be what you want to be—strength to keep God's good will for you and your life. Being "sifted" by Satan is too horrible to contemplate.

## Does the Holy Ghost Help?

Doctrine and Covenants 130:23. *A [person] may receive the Holy Ghost, and it may descend upon him and not tarry with him.*

Did you know that? How many confirmations have you seen of little eight-year-olds who are freshly baptized? They've made covenants with Jesus, literally, promised to take upon themselves his name (and therefore his work and his will). Those having the authority from God and who hold the Melchizedek Priesthood lay their hands upon the young person's head, and in the name of Jesus Christ they bestow the gift of the Holy Ghost as they say, "Receive the Holy Ghost." That's a great line, a sacred blessing—if only the new member of the church will do as bidden, "receive the Holy Ghost!" But not everyone does, you see, as the above scripture reminds us.

The Holy Ghost cannot—repeat, *cannot*—dwell in an unclean being. Water and oil don't mix—that's an eternal law of nature. The Holy Ghost cannot function where there is wickedness or disobedience before God. And if you don't have the Holy Ghost, it's a big loss. The Holy Ghost, remember, witnesses that Jesus is the Christ, the Son of God, and the Creator. The Holy Ghost also warns of danger, instructs in sacred knowledge, and helps the individual discern right from wrong. This is an awesome blessing from God.

We're talking keep clean, keep the commandments, keep smart with the help of the Holy Ghost. To do anything else when you are in a position to function with such blessings—to do anything else is the ultimate stupidity.

## Your Cutting Edge

1 Timothy 4:14. *Neglect not the gift that is in thee, which was given thee by prophecy, with the laying on of the hands of the presbytery.*

That's it. You know it now!

With an edge like the gift of the Holy Ghost in your being, you can live a life worthy of a true disciple of Christ. You can become like him. You can be happy and satisfied and productive, no matter what life dumps on you through no fault of your own.

*NJO NJO NJO NJO NJO NJO NJO NJO NJO NJO*

# What Can You Do?

1 Timothy 4:12. *Let no [one] despise thy youth; but be thou an example of the believers, in word, in conversation, in charity, in spirit, in faith, in purity.*

As you become more and more like Jesus Christ, you speak properly and pleasingly; you avoid thoughtless comments, blasphemous humor, and filthy swearing. Your conversation is positive, uplifting, and without lies. You are filled with charity, or quality caring (love, if you will), for others of Heavenly Father's family. You want to help! You want to make a difference. You are filled with the Spirit. You teach adults about faith instead of doubt. You are pure, a true example of one who can live in the world of low life and not partake of it.

# Here's the Promise!

Alma 5:33. *Behold, he sendeth an invitation unto all men, for the arms of mercy are extended towards them, and he saith: Repent, and I will receive you.*

These things are true—all the scriptures we've included here! And the blessing of it all is that Christ is waiting to encircle us in his arms. I mean, is that good enough! Think of the towering Christus statue at Temple Square in Salt Lake City, Utah. Picture yourself caught up in the arms of such a manly, kindly, loving being!

If you happen to be in the area of the temple in Washington, D.C., see if it is possible for you to look at the wall-to-wall, ceiling-to-floor mural of the second coming of Christ. It is a stunner. All the peoples of the earth are pictured there—all races, royalty and simple folk, the whole and the lame, young and old. They are in the presence of the resurrected Christ, whose arms are outstretched. Those who have followed after him and worked toward perfection are at his right and are in the light reflecting from his welcoming being. At his left are all the rest—in darkness. They are weeping and wailing and gnashing their teeth, for they knew him not and are outside his welcome.

What a pity that "they knew him not." What a sadness when putting off a sweet and saving relationship deprives you of power. Why, it is like the athlete who is bumped from the team because of breaking training rules; or the student who fails high school and later wonders what happened to college.

Get close to the Lord—now! Find your way to him. He's the best friend you can ever have on earth or in heaven.

**NJO NJO NJO NJO NJO NJO NJO NJO NJO NJO**

# CHAPTER
## 12

*Your Best Friend*
*on Earth or*
*in Heaven*

# *Your Best Friend on Earth or in Heaven*

Everybody needs a friend. We're talking real friends—loyal, caring, true and tender, forgiving, serving, a sharing lender.

Consider these insights on friendship from famous people of earlier times:

Benjamin Franklin claimed that "there are three faithful friends—an old wife, an old dog, and ready money." Well, that let's you out. You really are not ready for that point of view, are you?

Anacharsis, on the other hand, wrote that it was better to have just one friend of great value than many friends who are good for nothing.

Surely by now you have learned in some English class or on a greeting card, perhaps, that a friend is someone who loves you anyway, and that the only way to have a friend is to be one. Many prose and poetry artists from Emerson to Engelbert, in our day, have expressed similar lines.

*NJO NJO NJO NJO NJO NJO NJO NJO NJO NJO*

Napoleon Bonaparte, of all people, was a man who was hard-pressed to find someone he could trust, let alone someone who would love him "anyway." But he had a noble idea about friendship that is worth considering. Said Bonaparte, "A faithful friend is a true image of Deity."

In other words, the person who is most like the Lord in kindly traits, loving ways, and quality of character is the person you would most like for a close friend. You want to be able to count on such a friend as being unchanging, always there for you.

Why not start at the top? Become a friend of Jesus.

You want the best in friendship as well as life—go for it! Start building a choice relationship with the Lord and other things will likely fall into proper place and pleasing proportions for you.

The best friend you can ever have on earth or in heaven is the Lord Jesus Christ. There aren't many in the world who understand this, but you **not just ordinary** Young Men and Young Women had better get hold of this idea and fast.

The thousands of nonscriptural books that tell the story of Jesus usually are caught up in boring repetitions, dogmatic proofs, and learned discussions. You can read about him in the world's literature, though there are few which seek to give food fit for the soul and enlightenment for your very special needs today. You will have to find your own way to a meaningful relationship with the Savior. Church programs and ordinances are an incredible blessing in this pursuit. Of course, you'll need to listen to the instruction, the ordinance prayers (like the sacrament prayers), the testimonies and experiences of others, too. You'll need to heed the promptings and listen to the enlightenment from the Holy Ghost that fills your mind and heart.

*NJO  NJO  NJO  NJO  NJO  NJO  NJO  NJO  NJO  NJO*

Seek the Savior. Learn of him by study but also by faith. Follow him and prove him a living, caring, creator; a friend who knows your name and your earthly purpose; a perfect being—a God!—who cares about your heartaches and your struggles to surmount temptation.

You will find your friend when first you recognize him in all his extraordinary, loving vividness; listen to and live by the countless teachings he gives that are precisely suited to you, relevant for your time and situation in life. You will come to believe that he lives still and relates to us as intimately as he did to those disciples who moved with him about Galilee and Judea.

No doubt you will find in this chapter some things you have heard before about the Lord Jesus Christ. But in this setting I would like to remind you of those particular things which are important to you now, that will change your life. This chapter should be more than a beautiful part in a good book. When it comes to talking about Christ, it is my desire that you feel his presence, witness his wonder as a creator, and come to a rising commitment that you want, *in fact*, to become like him, as he indicated.

You are young and privileged, educated and advantaged (which has little to do with money), lively in spiritual things, and full of imaginations. You seem to really see things not only as they are but also as they might be. You might be like the people described by Giovanni Papini, a humble Italian student and writer about the Savior: "The man of imagination sees everything as though it were new: every great star, wheeling in the night, might lead you to the house hiding the Son of God; every stable has a manger which, filled with dry hay and clean straw, might become a cradle; every bare mountain top flaming with light in the golden mornings above the still somber valley, might be Sinai or Mt. Tabor: in the fires in the stubble, or in the charcoal kilns shining on the evening hills you can see the flame lighted by God to guide you in the desert. . . The dove cooing on the edge of the slate roof is . . . the same that descended on the waters of the Jordan."[16]

The following poem is worth memorizing—something to think about when your spirits are high or your mood is dragging; when you want to program garbage music or language out of your mind and replace it with inspiration. This poem is described as the testimony of the great Simon Peter, Apostle of the Lord Jesus in Jerusalem.

### The Boat

I owned a little boat a while ago,
And sailed the morning sea without a fear,
And whither any breeze might fairly blow
I steered my little craft afar or near.
    Mine was the boat
    And mine the air,
    And mine the sea,
    Nor mine a care.

My boat became my place of mighty toil,
I sailed at evening to the fishing ground,
At morn my boat was freighted with the spoil
Which my all-conquering work had found.
    Mine was the boat
    And mine the net,
    And mine the skill
    And power to get.

*NJO NJO NJO NJO NJO NJO NJO NJO NJO NJO*

One day there came along that silent shore,
While I my net was casting in the sea,
A Man who spoke as never man before.
I followed Him; new life began in me.
>Mine was the boat,
>But His the voice,
>And His the call,
>Yet mine the choice.

Ah! 'twas a fearful night out on the lake,
And all my skill availed not, at the helm,
Till Him asleep I waked, crying, "Take
Thou the helm—lest water overwhelm!"
>And His the boat,
>And His the sea,
>And His the peace
>O'er all and me.

Once from the boat He taught the curious throng
Then bade me cast my net into the sea;
I murmured but obeyed, nor was it long
Before the catch amazed and humbled me.
>His was the boat,
>And His the skill.
>And His the catch,
>And His my will.[17]

Once we begin our search to find the Lord and to find ourselves inextricably bound to him as friend and follower, we feel deep within us that he is not far from us—"for in him we live, and move, and have our being" (Acts 17:28). You see, we also are God's offspring. The Spirit within us "beareth witness with our spirit" that we are *in fact* the children of God (Romans 8:16). Jesus is our Elder Brother and has called us who believe in

*NJO NJO NJO NJO NJO NJO NJO NJO NJO NJO*

him "friends." He said, "Greater love hath no man than this, that a man lay down his life for his friends. Ye are my friends, if ye do whatsoever I command you. ... I have called you friends; for all things that I have heard of my Father I have made known unto you. Ye have not chosen me, but I have chosen you. ... These things I command you, that ye love one another." (John 15:13–17.)

Christ is the best friend we'll ever have on earth or in heaven.

He loves us anyway.

He laid down his life that we might live again after death.

He chose us and now we can choose him as a friend and strive to understand him. The more we learn of him, the more we value him. The more we keep his commandments, the greater is our understanding of our friendship, our love with him.

He calls you friends and says, in the Bible, that you no longer are just servants, because, as he teaches, he wouldn't tell a servant all that he has made known to you of Heavenly Father! If you ever forget just why you are **not ordinary** Young Men and Young Women, remember all that Jesus has shown us of God, our Heavenly Father.

Jesus was, in mortal life, the one perfect man to walk the earth among God's children. He is the best possible example for us in how we should try to treat others and respond to ill treatment and be sensitive to others' needs and be helpful with regard to their weaknesses.

No one else has taught such wonderful truths so clearly. No one else has made such an incredible sacrifice nor promised us a comparable hope of joy now and forever. No one else has said he would take our burdens upon his back, even so that we can't feel them ourselves right while we're suffering. And imagine, he has done just that, time after time, and will again if we'll turn to him.

For that reason alone I would claim Jesus to be the best friend I could ever have.

Our friends and family may love us and be helpful, but none can do what Christ can do!

Never doubt that he lives—that he lives and functions and governs that and those (you, too!) which he created under the direction of Heavenly Father. A truly exciting scripture in Doctrine and Covenants 76 reminds us that "by him, and through him, and of him, the worlds are and were created, and the inhabitants thereof are begotten sons and daughters unto God" (v. 24).

That is true. Now apply this to your particular life and age. You need a friend when your heart is breaking because you feel as if you don't "fit in," or the one you dream about has just fallen in love with someone else, or you become paralyzed in a wreck just before you are to rate raves as an athlete, or you suddenly find yourself a burn victim in an industrial accident, or you are miserable in your home life for whatever reason and no one seems to care.

Sometimes you may be relentlessly and terribly tempted. You don't know what to do—mother is at home, your favorite seminary teacher isn't around, and there is no escape except through your own will and action and that seems impossible under the circumstances. But always remember and *believe* that there is one who *can* help. Who but Jesus can support you, inspire you, protect you? When you draw near to him, he will draw near to you.

When you are young in today's world and **not just**

NJO  NJO  NJO  NJO  NJO  NJO  NJO  NJO  NJO  NJO

an **ordinary** Young Man or Young Woman, you are marked by the devil. You are known to the forces of evil. You are targeted as one whose life should be ruined so that you will be ineffective, so that you can't help others in your age-group behave as they should, keeping God's commandments for all the right reasons. Christ lives and is waiting to be gracious to you. Remember, too, that Satan is a being who also yearns to have an influence over you. Unlike that of your friend and Savior, Jesus Christ, Satan's influence is ruinous.

It is easy to be good when you are home and safe in bed, but out in the world, where people don't understand, it is another matter. Keep in mind Daniel, who was a prisoner and wouldn't eat and drink items on the king's menu. He wanted to keep what might be called the Word of Wisdom of his day, and he prayed to God for help. He was helped and rose to a high place in the kingdom helping others. And David, who slew Goliath with God's help amid the tauntings of the great Philistine army. And Joseph, sold into Egypt, who wanted security in the palace of the Pharaoh but chose to flee rather than succumb to the enticings of a woman. Or Joseph Smith, who put his hand in God's, who trusted his friend-above-earthly-friends, even Jesus Christ, and was indeed helped to withstand the persecution of disbelievers and people overcome by Satan's influence.

And here is a scripture that is comforting as well as true, and that underscores the idea that Jesus is your best friend, in the best sense of the phrase, on earth or in heaven: "Be strong and of a good courage; be not afraid, neither be thou dismayed: for the Lord thy God [and thy friend] is with thee whithersoever thou goest" (Joshua 1:9).

*NJO NJO NJO NJO NJO NJO NJO NJO NJO NJO*

## You'll Want to Remember . . .

Aspects of a good relationship with God would include the following:

- *Know* what he wants you to do and be and become.
- *Pray* to him at the same time daily for a formal contact, and turn your thoughts to him all during the day to help you be like he is, to resist temptation, to do your best in school or at work or performing.
- *Bear witness* to others when moved upon by the Spirit—that Christ did atone for you (and others), that God does hear and answer prayers.
- *Love* him and love his children.

The infinite love of God is beautifully described in the scripture found in Romans 8:38–39: "For I am persuaded, that neither death, nor life, nor angels, nor principalities, nor powers, nor things present, nor things to come, nor height, nor depth, nor any other creature, shall be able to separate us from the love of God, which is in Christ Jesus our Lord."

With the Lord as your friend your satisfaction in life is guaranteed.

*NJO NJO NJO NJO NJO NJO NJO NJO NJO NJO*

# CHAPTER
## 13

# *Satisfaction Guaranteed*

# Satisfaction Guaranteed

There was a boy whose room was the local disaster area. Before self-destruct time happened, his mother took a stand. In the doorway, she was, like a five-foot-four giant colossus, and her words sounded as if she meant what she said.

"Son, you and I have a problem."

"Oh? What is that?"

"Your room couldn't even pass for a yard sale."

"That bad, huh?"

"That bad, son."

"Well, Mom, did you want to have a garage sale?"

"No, sweetness, I do not want to have a garage sale. I want you to clean your room—like new."

"Well, it's my room, so forget it."

"Well, it's my house and I can't forget it."

"So that's the problem?"

"You got it! Now, clean up your room—FAX-fast."

"But Mom, I am only one person."

"Who would ever believe that? There are enough socks under that bed to—"

"Yeah, yeah—to clothe an army."

"You have heard that before."

"Right."

"You will not hear it again. The next thing you hear will be the sound of your guitar crashing against your head."

"Mother! I am shocked!"

"I am, too, by the sight of your room. Use your free agency and get this place safe."

"Free agency?"

"Free agency."

"What does that have to do with socks under the bed?"

"Just this—you choose to live like a pig and you get to live with the—"

"Relax, Mom. I am way ahead of you. This cluttered room is already history."

"Son, you are not just an ordinary boy. I am thankful for you and that you get the picture. I expect satisfaction guaranteed—in the room cleanup and with all the rest of your life."

This boy was right, in his way. He was only one. And so are you, but this is your stretch of the turf, your time to sing your song. What you do with your time, what you choose to become, includes, of course, keeping your quarters clean, but this is only the beginning.

You know that this stage of life, with the challenges that you face and the expectations adults have for you, is only the beginning. Today, the very wise say, is the first day of all the rest of your life. Whatever it is to be is up to you. Fortify yourself and go for the altogether prize. Pray, prepare to live well and contribute much and perform—do it!

*NJO NJO NJO NJO NJO NJO NJO NJO NJO NJC*

Consider these lines from E. E. Cummings: "To be nobody-but-yourself—in a world which is doing its best, night and day, to make you everybody else— means to fight the hardest battle which any human being can fight; and never stop fighting."[18]

That's it. No rest for the **not just ordinary** Young Men and Young Women. But the rewards are awesome, and the satisfaction is guaranteed—if only you'll continue to grow up wonderful.

# Notes

1. Phrase used in First Presidency introduction to *For the Strength of Youth* [booklet] (Salt Lake City: The Church of Jesus Christ of Latter-day Saints, 1990), p. 3.

2. Will and Ariel Durant, *The Lessons of History* (New York: Simon and Schuster, 1968), p. 34.

3. William Shakespeare, *Hamlet*, act 2, scene 2, lines 536–38.

4. First Presidency, introduction to *For the Strength of Youth*, p. 3.

5. See *Ensign* 17 (April 1987): 73.

6. William Wordsworth, "Character of the Happy Warrior," in *The Oxford Authors: William Wordsworth*, ed. Stephen Gill (Oxford: Oxford University Press, 1984), p. 320.

7. Emily Dickinson, "If I Can Stop One Heart from Breaking," in *Masterpieces of Religious Verse*, ed. James Dalton Morrison (New York: Harper and Row, 1948), p. 418.

8. First Presidency, introduction to *For the Strength of Youth*, pp. 4–5.

9. Spencer W. Kimball, "Privileges and Responsibilities of Sisters," *Ensign* 8 (November 1978): 104.

10. Spencer W. Kimball, *One Silent Sleepless Night* (Salt Lake City: Bookcraft, 1975), p. 5.

11. Kimball, *Sleepless Night*, pp. 23–26.

12. Miguel de Cervantes, *Don Quixote*, Ormsby translation, ed. Joseph R. Jones and Kenneth Douglas, Norton critical edition (New York: W. W. Norton & Company, 1981), p. 103.

13. Words spoken by Marcus Antonius in William Shakespeare, *Julius Caesar*, act 3, scene 2, line 75.

14. Mark Twain, *The Adventures of Huckleberry Finn*, Bantam Classic edition (New York: Bantam, 1981), p. 205.

15. Bruce R. McConkie, *Mormon Doctrine*, 2d ed. (Salt Lake City: Bookcraft, 1966), pp. 548–49.

16. Giovanni Papini, *Life of Christ*, trans. Dorothy Canfield Fisher (New York: Harcourt, Brace and Company, 1923), pp. 13–14.

17. George Macdonald, "The Boat," in *Masterpieces of Religious Verse*, ed. James Dalton Morrison (New York: Harper and Row, 1948), p. 176.

18. E. E. Cummings, *E. E. Cummings: A Miscellany Revised*, ed. George J. Firmage (New York: October House Inc., 1965), p. 335.

*NJO  NJO  NJO  NJO  NJO  NJO  NJO  NJO  NJO  NJC*